C000130833

On the Golf Tour

On
the
Golf
Tour

A *Journeyman*
Professional's
Story

IAN and DON MOSEY

With a Foreword by
PETER ALLISS

Methuen London

To Jo
Mother and Wife

First published in Great Britain 1989
by Methuen London Ltd
Michelin House, 81 Fulham Road, London sw3 6rb
Copyright © 1989 Ian and Don Mosey

Photoset by Rowland Phototypesetting Ltd
Bury St Edmunds, Suffolk
Printed in Great Britain
by Mackays of Chatham plc,
Chatham, Kent

A CIP catalogue record for this book is available
from the British Library

ISBN 0 413 61340 2

Contents

Illustrations

The photographs in this book are reproduced by kind permission of Bob Bird, *Liverpool Daily Post*: 2; Phil Sheldon: 3a, 3b, 4a, 4b, 5a, 5b, 8a, 8b. Illustrations 6a, 6b, 7a, 7b were drawn by Shaun Williams.

Foreword

It gives me great pleasure to write this foreword to Don and Ian Mosey's book. The reasons may not be readily obvious, but I have to tell you that the Alliss family has had close associations with the wondrous game of cricket for more than seventy years.

Why? you may be thinking. Well, on returning from active service with the Argyll and Sutherland Highlanders during the First World War my father, Percy, applied for a trial with Yorkshire County Cricket Club, but at the same time sent off a letter asking to be considered for the post of assistant professional with Jock Hutchinson at the Royal Porthcawl Golf Club in South Wales. Suffice it to say that the letter from Porthcawl arrived before the one from Yorkshire CCC and so golf, instead of cricket, became my father's life.

Now, we've had autobiographies of top golfers, instructional books and statistical surveys, books on great golf courses and many on where to play. But I don't think there has ever been a book from what you might call a bread-and-butter golfer, one whose life is spent playing the game all the year round, who makes a decent living without ever really threatening – or indeed expecting – to win the Open Championship, and all without a club professional's job to fall back on.

What does it take to make it at this level? What sort of effort is involved in equipping oneself to make money playing in competition with the top stars of world golf? How much work goes into it? What are the essential differences between top amateur golf and the professional circuit? What are the snags, the dangers? How many fall by the wayside each year and why does this happen? Are they glad they at least made the attempt at crossing over the golfing Jordan to the Promised Fairway? These are some of the questions answered in this book.

I find it fascinating as I, too, have watched Ian Mosey's career and seen how often he has been so nearly 'there'. At thirty-eight years of age, perhaps he will not now show any great signs of improvement, but who knows – wasn't Ben Hogan thirty years of age before he had any real signs of success?

This book illustrates a unique father-and-son partnership and tells of the professional effort Ian has put into his game. I am sure his father has fussed around him busily as my father fussed around me, always anxious as a parent whether he was doing the right thing – was the boy practising hard enough? Was he making a total effort to learn his trade? In fact, desperate to put an old head on young shoulders.

But this is not a book of grim intensity. It contains a wealth of anecdote from both co-authors. Don is a club golfing enthusiast of the very best sort, but known to so many Radio 3 listeners as a lively member of the BBC commentary team, the wonderful 'Test Match Special', and someone who has also covered nineteen Open Championships on radio as well as many other premier golfing events.

So there you have it. This is a warm insight into the camaraderie and (dare one say?) chivalry of a game which may well be sport's last bastion of good manners and gentlemanly conduct. Although there are one or two cracks in the old superstructure, I hope it will be a long time before this funny old game disintegrates as many others have done so dramatically over the past twenty years or so. As many of my old golfing friends would say, 'Take the book and enjoy.'

Peter Alliss

1   *Cricket? No, Golf!*

Don: Ian James Mosey was born on 29 August 1951, a truly propitious moment according to the soothsayers since Bob Appleyard, the Yorkshire bowler, had just taken his 200th wicket in his first full season of county cricket. As young Ian James was specifically and very specially intended to play that game for the county of his birth, the stars seemed to be in a favourable orbit. His mother had been despatched to Yorkshire to stay with her parents three months before the baby was due to arrive. We were taking no chances on his (there was absolutely no question of a 'her') being born on unhallowed ground. When it was reported to the father, working on a newspaper in Nottingham, that his lady wife had ventured on a day trip *to Blackpool* a matter of days before the projected date of birth, the enormity of the risk she had taken sent him into deep shock.

Within hours of the birth, telegrams started arriving from friends and colleagues in Nottingham: 'Have booked seats for Trent Bridge Test, 1971', 'Have ordered size one bat from Gunn and Moore.' Many of them referred to the child as, 'Len Don Herbert,' the forenames designated (according to father) long before he was born which would ensure that he could not possibly fail as a batsman. So bizarre were some of the messages that someone in Keighley Post Office telephoned to ask what was happening. The answer was quite simple – a new Yorkshire cricketer of the future had been born – and no further information was required by the caller. These things are (or used to be) readily understood in the county of the broad acres.

Ian: I can't remember exactly when it was that I realised my destiny lay on the cricket fields of Headingley, Park Avenue and beyond. There was a sort of dawning consciousness that something special was expected of me, even though I was not pushed in any particular sporting direction as far as coaching was concerned. I was taken to watch Dad play on Saturdays, and some Sundays as well, and when we went on our summer holidays a ball was always involved in our seaside games. Gradually – painfully for some – it became clear that I had no aptitude whatsoever for the game of cricket! It also began to emerge that I had nothing like the necessary co-ordination to play rugby – or even soccer – either. The sporting future was beginning to look rather bleak, but still no pressure was put on me at this stage as far as sport was concerned. On academic matters, however, it was a different story.

I had private coaching to help get me through the eleven-plus examination. Pressure to carry out extra study at home was incessant, and though I did not regard the eleven-plus as having any great significance in my life my father appeared to look upon it as the most important event to occur so far. When I missed out on a grammar school place his disappointment was transcended only by his fury at what he saw as a lack of effort on my part. I couldn't even compensate by showing a leaning of any kind towards sport. I was a rather unhappy eleven-year-old.

Don: I spent hours trying to rationalise the situation, telling myself that it was unfair to expect to fulfil one's own ambitions through one's children. To bolster my belief that I *was* being fair I carefully avoided pressuring Ian towards any particular sporting goal. This, however, served to strengthen my belief that a good standard of education was essential, and that meant a university place and a degree. How could he hope to progress on those lines if he couldn't get into a grammar school? Alas, Ian was a frail and sickly child, plagued by asthma since he was a baby and beset by the parallel problems of eczema. I had had a similar childhood and been mercilessly bullied, notably by two brothers from a Roman Catholic School which lay on my route home from my Church of England School. This was not in Belfast but in the West Yorkshire town of Keighley and to this day I automatically react to the discovery that any acquaintance follows the teachings of Rome, so profound was the experience of my earliest schooldays. I desperately wanted to shield Ian from any possibility of a similar experience. In the sprawling urban mass of Manchester, where we moved when he was six years old, this looked like being difficult to achieve.

After much searching, I found a private school in Heaton Moor, sandwiched between Manchester and Stockport, where I hoped he would get a better quality of tuition as well as a chance of freedom from persecution for his frailty. It was not long before I realised I had made a mistake on the first count; it was many years before my son informed me I had also been wrong on the second. But at least it was during his time at Heaton Moor College that Ian (quite suddenly, it seemed) began to manifest an interest in sport – in golf.

My wife had played the game since she was a child, and with Denton Golf Club only a few minutes away from our home I began to dabble with the game myself. During a family holiday on Burgh Island, off the Devon coast, in 1963, I was persuaded to hack my way around the neighbouring Bigbury-on-Sea course and young Ian walked round with his parents and a ball and a putter to keep him amused. That was the day the first seeds were sown. On our return to Manchester and in his first year at Heaton Moor College he began to spend holidays and weekends at Denton Golf Club, searching for hours in the luxuriant 'rough' for lost golf balls. In a remarkably short space of time he had accumulated a store of them and by far his favourite pastime now became a daily counting of the golf balls, gloating over them and grading them according to condition. For the next two or three years of Ian's life, that plastic bag of golf balls became his most treasured possession. He was just twelve years old when he announced that he would like to learn to play golf.

Ian: I was presented to the Denton pro, Brian Allen, who found me a half-set of ladies' clubs, the lightest he had around, and gave me a series of lessons so that I started on the right foot with the basics of the game. From that moment, every spare moment of school holidays was spent at Denton Golf Club. When I was allowed, as a very junior junior, to play the full course, I played it. When I was not allowed on the course I stood on the practice ground trying to remember what the pro had told me. The idea was beginning to form in my mind that this might be what I wanted to do as a career. I *liked* golf; I didn't like school. My father loved journalism and my mother felt the same way about teaching. Why shouldn't I spend my working life doing something *I* loved? It all seemed very easy to me – not the golf but the philosophy.

Don: Ian's school examination results, which had never been impressive, now began to be pretty dire. When I inquired of the teaching staff what the problem was, I was told: 'Ian says he's going to spend his life playing golf; it's not necessary for him to learn anything here.' Really? Was this why I was paying fees I couldn't really afford to shelter my first-born from the harsh reality of life in a secondary modern? A rather grim father-and-son discussion took place, as a result of which Ian was removed from his private school and went to Egerton Park Secondary Modern, where he at least went through the motions of academic study and, to my astonishment, seemed a good deal happier than he had been at the other place. My end of the bargain was that at fifteen he could leave school and start work on his chosen career as a golfer. I would place him totally in the pro's keeping for a year, at the end of which Brian Allen's verdict would be binding on us both. If Brian said Ian had the makings of a golfer I would do everything I could to help; if Brian gave the thumbs-down he would have to face life as one of the thousands of job-hunters with no qualifications.

There had to be a snag, of course, and it came at my end of the partnership. In August 1964 I was writing cricket for the *Daily Mail* and doing a couple of broadcasts a week into North Regional sports programmes. The Yorkshire team, who were my friends as well as some of the people I wrote about, asked me to help in organising a September–October tour to the USA and Canada. Brian Close, the captain, and I sat down to work things out and in a month we had raised the money to make the tour possible. I would go with them, probably play in a couple of the games and make a film of the trip which would become the *Daily Mail* cricket show, to be staged at club and league functions during the winter. In those days I never went into the office in Manchester during the summer and so it came as a complete shock to learn via the telephone that 'London (head office) had turned down the idea of my going with the tourists.' To make it worse, my colleagues of the *Express* and *Mirror were* going on the trip which would take in New York, Vancouver, Hollywood and Bermuda – the holiday of a lifetime.

I was bitterly disappointed but every telephoned inquiry to my editor and sports editor in Manchester brought the same answer: London had turned it down and there was nothing they could do about it. Unknown to me, Close and the Yorkshire team then wrote to Bill Hicks, the London sports editor of the *Daily Mail*, asking him to change his mind and approve my trip. During a game at Sheffield, Close showed me a letter from Hicks. It said he knew nothing about the proposal and would have been glad to approve it if he *had* known. It was something of a body blow to find I had been let down by a man who was not merely my editor but a personal friend. I brooded over this for a few days, then, on Saturday 15 August, I sent two telegrams – one to Freddie Trueman congratulating him on taking his 300th Test wicket at the Oval, the other to the *Daily Mail* announcing that at the end of the current game (Sussex *v.* Yorkshire at Hove) I would be driving back north and re-signing. I did so, and with a wife and two growing boys, one with the ambition to be a full-time golfer, I put myself out of a job.

It was sixteen weeks before I found a job I wanted to do. I could have gone to one paper which I didn't fancy; the paper I did fancy had no immediate vacancy. I could have made a decent living freelancing as writer and broadcaster but I was constitutionally unsuited to that sort of hit-and-miss existence. In December 1964 I joined the BBC and my income, from what it had been with the *Daily Mail*, was almost exactly halved! A £2,000-a-year salary plus two broadcasts a week at five guineas a time now became a salary of £1,300 and no broadcasting fees. It had also been possible to make a fair profit on my newspaper expenses, especially when travelling the summer cricket circuit; that had now gone. When Ian left school there would be no tax relief, even though I would then be responsible for his 'further education'. If he were in a college, *costing* the taxpayers money, I would get relief; unfortunately there were no colleges with courses for aspiring golfers. And soon his younger brother would (we hoped) have passed *his* eleven-plus and would require financial support at grammar school. It was not going to be easy.

Ian: Knowing little of all this – and I doubt whether I would have understood its implications in any case – I was delighted with the idea of devoting all my time to golf. By now I was enthusiastic about the game and the more I learned of its mysteries from Brian Allen the more fascinated I became. For the first time in my life I had found something on which I could really concentrate and which I could enjoy at the same time. There was little opportunity for competitive golf at Denton, but I joined Manchester and District Junior Golf Society, with whom I could play in competitions organised by one or two senior players, to whom I am sure we were not properly grateful. With all the arrogance of youth we regarded it as our right to have competitions arranged and for courses to be made available to us. It was all necessary to put a competitive edge on our golf and we did not look much further than that. But at least my parents were firmly behind me. Even Dad seemed to have recovered from the shock of discovering that I was not gifted academically and was now vigorously backing my golfing apprenticeship. Over in Yorkshire, at the club where mother had learned *her* golf, a venerable old chap called Bert Jolly was practising what I suppose would now be called a golf consultancy and he had a great reputation as a teacher. I was now taken to see him.

Don: Bert Jolly had been a member of the first Ryder Cup team and on occasional visits to the Branshaw Club, high on the moors above Keighley, I had enjoyed chatting to him, particularly about his trip to the USA in 1927. He had, I suppose one might say, fallen on hard times in later years but was now enjoying a certain vogue as a teacher. In fact club golfers came from miles around to see him and when I learned that amongst those who consulted him was Rodney Foster, the Walker Cup player from the Bradford Club, I thought his views on Ian's potential might well be valuable. Branshaw Golf Club was a strange place to find a distinguished teacher and former top pro. It was not at that time a club in the Wentworth or Sunningdale mould – not at all. The clubhouse was a ramshackle wooden structure where conversation in one room was perfectly audible in the next. The locker rooms (or rather, the toilets) were side by side and separated only by a mere thickness of planking. This had caused one captain to put up a notice (pretty certainly at the behest of his wife!) in the gents which was as graphic as it was ungrammatical: 'Please do not fart as the ladies can hear them.'

No – Branshaw was nothing like Wentworth or Sunningdale. But the course covered a wonderful sweep of moorland between one small river valley and the next, carpeted with heather and flanked by pinewoods. The views ranged from the purple expanse of Brontëland to the broadening of Airedale under the shadow of Ilkley Moor. A sunny afternoon on the Branshaw course was a sheer delight and so it made a pleasant outing to subject Ian to the Bert Jolly scrutiny. He looked attentively at the mechanics of our son's golf, made encouraging noises, and we returned to Manchester that evening with all the satisfaction of Greeks who had consulted the Dephic Oracle and received an optimistic forecast.

Ian: Mr Jolly was well over eighty when that first meeting took place and to me that seemed quite incredibly ancient. I don't think I had even heard of the Ryder Cup at that time and the fact that he had played in the first one made me wonder just what use the visit could possibly be. How could a man of that vintage relate to a teenager's golf? But my folks seemed to think it was worthwhile and I had played once or twice round the Branshaw course in the past. I didn't mind *where* I played so long as it was a golf course of some kind, and while I would probably have been happier spending Sunday afternoon on the practice ground at Denton (with a round with one of my friends once the course had cleared of members), at least the parental attitude was one of sweetness and light as we drove back home. With the considerable help of competitions arranged by the Junior Society, and being allowed to take part in occasional club competitions (providing I did not take a prize!) at Denton, I began to make some progress and by 1966, when I was fifteen my handicap was down to single figures (nine, in fact).

Don: Thinking that some sort of encouragement was called for, I suggested that Ian and I should go to Scotland for a week's golf in that warm and pleasant summer.

Ian: This was an exciting prospect. Apart from annual visits to Moor Park for the Carris Boys' Week, I had not played much golf at all outside the north of England and certainly never in

Scotland. Now I started to think about St Andrews and
Muirfield, Turnberry and Troon. It didn't work out quite like
that . . .

Don: I have been deeply fond of Scotland and the Scots since
I was a schoolboy, and this was the perfect opportunity to mix
pleasure with pleasure. We drove up the A9, stopping for a
round at Newtonmore, and made our base in a farmhouse just
south of Nairn. For a week we played Nairn Dunbar, breaking
off occasionally for forays to Forres, Inverness and Carrbridge,
but generally the time was spent going round and round and
round the Dunbar course. As we finished at the eighteenth
green, Ian walked straight across to the first tee, ready to start
again. When he did this for the second time, on the second day,
the time had come to call a halt. I was still only a dabbler at the
game and both hands and feet were beginning to feel a bit sore.
Also, after half a dozen rounds on the holiday I had lost about
two dozen brand new Wilson Staffs balls in gorse thickets, and
as a 'careful' Yorkshireman I found this intolerable. Towards
the end of the week I was doing one round and leaving Ian to
cram in two more and sometimes three.

In northern Scotland it stays light until very late in mid-
summer. One day I drove over to Skye, on another I sat on
Culloden battlefield – that most evocative of British historical
sites – while my son and heir blasted his way gaily around the
Dunbar course in a way which seemed to have excited the
admiration of the locals. Never had anyone got so much value
for his green fees on their course, even if he was a Sassenach. On
the Friday I returned from an excursion to find small son
waiting for me with shining eyes. He had been invited to play
for the Dunbar club in an annual needle match against Forres.
Was it all right with me?

I telephoned my wife with the tidings that her first-born was
enjoying himself hugely, that I was nearly dead from exhaus-
tion and that we would rejoin her and number two son the
following evening in Morecambe, where we were to enjoy a
brief *family* holiday. After a pint or two in Nairn I returned to
the Dunbar club to take my son to bed, only to be faced with a
wait of an hour while victory over Forres was celebrated. Father
sat in the car park listening to 'Friday Night is Music Night'

while son (winner of his match by six and five) was fed on salmon salad and chips. We returned south the following day, a blazing hot Saturday, listening to a description of England's World Cup victory over West Germany by my friend and colleague, Alan Clarke.

Ian: By the time I was legally able to leave school and get on with what was now the real purpose of life, my own personality had changed quite a bit. With a definite future ahead of me (I never thought for one second that I might not make it in my coach's eyes when he delivered his verdict to father) I even enjoyed to some extent the last few months at school. I made more friends than it had been possible to do when I was younger because I now had a more buoyant and optimistic outlook. I suppose I had reached a pretty low ebb at the time I was cramming unsuccessfully for the eleven-plus and then wasting my time at the private school. My relationship with the old man was a pretty tense one because he was convinced that I was a lot brighter than my school results indicated and he believed, therefore, that I was deliberately idling my way through adolescence. Physical retribution for my trans-gressions – real or imagined – would have been infinitely better than the tongue-lashings I suffered. Dad has always had a colourful turn of phrase and I got the full force of it on many occasions. I used to shudder at the prospect of the next one.

Once we had settled on the one-year-to-prove-myself deal and the pressure was off me to get good school results, I relaxed and life seemed altogether more pleasant. Even so, I slipped up occasionally. One Sunday afternoon he took brother Andrew and me to the cinema – one of the costume spectaculars which all three of us enjoyed – and we were just settling down to enjoy the first battle scene when I suddenly went rigid. I shouldn't be there at all. I had a Junior Society match to play at three o'clock; it was now a quarter past. Dad, sitting between us, felt my tension and I had to confess. If we hadn't been in a cinema I have not the slightest doubt that his wrath would have taken on a physical, rather than merely verbal, manifestation. As a matter of fact, I think he was literally speechless with fury. Andrew (who, all his life, has refused to acknowledge that fear is acceptable in any context) opted to stay there alone and

watch the film while an infuriated father drove me three miles
up the road to Denton GC, where my opponent was patiently
waiting. Mercifully, I had won the match by the time the old
man had gone back to the cinema, been given a précis of what
he had missed and brought Andrew home. There was an icy
atmosphere in the old homestead that evening.

From the moment I left school, Denton Golf Club became my
workshop, and fortunately it had one of the largest practice
areas in the district. To most of the members, Brian Allen was a
trifle grim and unsmiling. Indeed, I have known him tell
members who came for lessons to stop wasting *his* time and *their*
money because they would never make golfers. This from a club
pro whose major source of income was the lessons he gave! But
he would never suffer fools gladly under any circumstances. He
played a certain amount of tournament golf himself and could
usually be relied upon to return at least one low round which
indicated that technically he was a very accomplished player.
To me he was magic. He sensed quite early that I meant it, that
I was determined to make a career in the game and was willing
to work as hard as he demanded. Apart from my official lessons,
he spent hours of his own time working with me; as long as I was
willing to listen and learn, Brian was willing to teach and in that
first year as a full-time learner-golfer my handicap came down
to four.

I think the happiest day of my life up to that point was when I
partnered him in a Manchester and District Alliance meeting
at Chapel-en-le-Frith and we won. A small paragraph in the
northern edition of the *Daily Telegraph* (a paper which does so
much for golf with its detailed coverage, and in other ways)
recorded that this was the first time a sixteen-year-old amateur
had partnered a pro to victory in such a competition. To me it
was simply my first opportunity to say a tangible 'thank you' to
Brian for all he was doing for me. One's first teacher can play a
vital part in any golfer's career and when he left the country to
take up a post at a country club in the USA I was, for a time,
lost. Whenever anything went wrong with my game I was
almost desperate to turn to Brian for help; I believed in him
utterly and completely. It was many years before I was able to
place such complete trust in a coach, and that was John Jacobs.

I had left my amateur apprenticeship far behind me and was well into my professional career when I turned in the late seventies to John. Ten or eleven years had gone by since I had had any expert tuition; mentally, I still relied on what Brian Allen had taught me and when he was 3,000 miles away, somehow I felt that no one else could tutor me in the way that he had done. Nothing I read, or saw on television, made sense to me in the light of what I'd learned from Brian, until I found Jacobs. I met him on a John Brown Engineering golf seminar at Meon Valley. These took place over three nights and four days in early spring or late autumn and they involved coaching, talks about the psychology of the game and hours and hours of practice. Almost without exception I came to make some of my best tournament scores immediately after one of those seminars. The Tunisian Open, for instance, was only staged four times and I finished eighth, seventh, fifty-fifth (!) and fifth and I went to those straight from one of Jacobs's coaching sessions. It was after another of them that I went to Australia and finished third in the New South Wales Open. Not only does it suggest that I could well have seen more of him during the really lean early years on the tournament circuit but I wish I could see more of him now. Fashions come and go in the teaching of the game and at various times several men have enjoyed a vogue but John Jacobs is, in my opinion, the most knowledgeable man on the golf swing. His depth of knowledge, commonsense approach and the ability to impart advice is outstanding. Whenever I am in trouble I go in search of him and hope he can find an hour or two to straighten me out.

Don: A year of solid hard work, building on the foundations laid by Brian Allen, in 1967 was followed by one in which the results began to show. At first the successes were local – a couple of wins at Denton, a Manchester Junior Society victory – and then a couple of course records at Denton and Hesketh (Southport) were followed by a round of 68 at Stockport which made him at last a Category One golfer. By July 1968, he and his friend Ian Bamborough (another Denton junior, later to become a club professional at Tenby, then Ganton, the great East Yorkshire course) had been called up for the England Boys' trials. First, however, came the British Boys' Championship at St Anne's Old Links where Steven Evans, the England Boys' captain, accounted for both the Denton youngsters – Bamborough in the fourth round, Mosey in the semi-final. I was delighted with the progress he had made in four golfing months of that year and my delight was complete when, in August, Ian was chosen for the England Boys' team to play against Scotland. We are a pretty undemonstrative pair and have never been able to talk to each other about closely personal matters, and this occasion was no exception. I wrote Ian a note telling him how proud he had made me, slipped a fiver into the envelope and to save us both what would have been an intensely embarrassing moment, left the note with his mother and went out for a pint! On the way I called to see Brian Allen to say the most heartfelt 'thank you'.

In his first international match, he partnered Warren Humphreys, then one of the outstanding young players in Britain. It was the start of a friendship which was to become increasingly close over the next twenty years and still endures despite massive changes in both those young lives. Their victory, by four and three, over R. P. Fyfe Jnr and S. G. Thomson represented Ian's first success at any significant level and it was followed by a singles win over R. T. Campbell by two holes. He reached his seventeenth birthday twelve days later, a very happy young man indeed.

Ian: By now I was growing stronger every year and a new set of clubs became necessary with embarrassing frequency. As the scope of my competitive golf had developed so dramatically during the past season, so had the necessity for more, and smarter, changes of golfing dress. If my father was keen that my clubs should be of the right size and weight, mother was equally determined that I should look the part of a junior international. It all cost money.

It was now time I started to take some of the financial strain, so I got some part-time work on the Denton course during the winter. The course was snowbound for much of the time and I dug ditches, felled old trees and carried out general labouring duties, practising now (when the weather allowed) during my lunch breaks. In the spring it was time to plant new saplings and, looking now at the Denton course, twenty years on, in all its arboreal splendour, I must say I think more of my aching back and blistered hands than of the enhanced appearance of the course. At Easter came the Carris Week, effectively the Boys' Stroke-Play Championship. I had been going there since I was fifteen, a slight and callow boy who remembered his delight when, on his first visit, he was allowed by Peter Dawson (an experienced and powerful left-hander from Woodhall Spa) to join him from a practice round. Two years is an eternity when you are a teenager and I did not dare allow myself to think that one day I would be, like Peter, a 'Carris boy' who played, in addition to the Championship itself, in the matches against the LGU girls and Dai Rees's team of professionals.

Now my moment had come – my last Carris before I moved on from boys' to youth golf, and I was still the least sophisticated member of that happy band of pilgrims which included Warren Humphreys, Ian Gradwell (my arch-rival in Lancashire boys' golf, later my partner in one or two ventures), Ian Bamborough from Denton and the one who seemed to me so much the young-man-about-town, John Putt, from Oxford City.

Don: And I remember particularly a young Nigel Sears, dapper and confident, who (when I was buying a round of pints of lemon-and-orange for the boys) asked if he might have a large Scotch. As I hesitated, the barman in Moor Park's palatial clubhouse resolved the matter with the crushing comment, 'No, you may not, *Master* Sears.' Nigel was game to the last. 'Are you suggesting I am not old enough to have a proper drink?' he demanded, with a fine haughtiness. 'Yes I am,' replied the steward. 'If you *were* old enough to have a drink you would not be playing in the Carris.' There was no answer to that.

There was much speculation on biological lines amongst the England boys on the eve of the match against the LGU girls. Ian, partnered by Kim Dabson, was drawn against the beauty of the girls' team, Beverley Huke (with Pamela Fitton), which all seemed a bit of a waste to the other boys. Ian would not have dreamed of asking the fair Beverley for a date, while most of his team-mates were panting for the opportunity to do so. Conversely, there was apprehension about who might have to cope with the bigger-hitting girls, who were playing off ladies' tees and getting five strokes. Still, apart from a bit of a snarl from the formidable Enid Wilson in the *Daily Telegraph* about slow play, it all passed very pleasantly and the girls won 6½ to 5½. The match against Dai Rees's professionals was a less social fixture with the boys, receiving four strokes apiece, very keen indeed to beat their senior opposition and doing so by ten matches to five. Carris Week when you are sixteen is great fun.

I do hope it is as enjoyable today (played at a later stage of the year with prospects of better weather) as it was when I drove Ian there for three years. I remember standing with Warren Humphreys's father and exchanging notes. 'Do you think we might have a spare shirt for our backs by the end of *this* year?' 'Do *you* realise that they will now both want their own car? They have had enough of being transported by the old man.' Remembering that particular exchange from the previous year, I now stopped the car at the entrance to the Moor Park estate and gave Ian the wheel so that he could drive up to the clubhouse for his final Carris Week. In some ways it was like one's final week at school – the end of one life and the beginning of a new one. I don't know whether Ian felt that way, but I certainly did. His boyhood was over.

'When Will He Get a Job?'

Ian: The new club professional at Denton at the start of 1969 was Eddie Birchenough, later to move on to Gog Magog in Cambridgeshire and then to Royal Lytham in time for the 1988 Open Championship to be staged there. He was an entirely different type from Brian Allen and we had a completely different, but extremely cordial, association. I had worshipped Brian; with Eddie I had a closer relationship in that we were really a couple of golfing pals, and yet he was helpful to me in many ways. We started the season by winning a Manchester and District Alliance meeting at Mere, and I was now called up by Lancashire Colts. This brought me into contact with Dr David Marsh, one of the country's leading amateurs and another man to whom I owe a deep debt of gratitude.

I also joined in a pro–am playing partnership with Noel Hunt, two years my senior, from the Fairfield Club which adjoins the Denton course in east Manchester. Fairfield is unusual in that it is a golf *and sailing* club, since it is handily laid out around a reservoir. Noel had been at Heaton Moor College at the same time as me and had bullied me mercilessly in the school which my father had found for me to avoid being bullied! Now that was forgotten as he turned professional with an attachment as an assistant at a driving range in Stockport, and together we played in a Whitbread-sponsored pro–am at Pleasington (Blackburn) and then in the Pannal Foursomes, where we made a bit of progress without setting the golfing world alight. By June I had reached the final of the Lancashire Amateur Championship, only to play absolute rubbish in the last round and lose by three and one. My driving was terribly off-target and having got so far I never gave myself a chance of becoming the youngest-ever county champion. It was back to the practice ground.

Don: By July, 1969, Ian was down to one handicap, but he was still just one of a bunch of fine young Lancashire golfers at that time – youngsters like Ian Gradwell, Andrew Chandler, Stephen Rooke, Nigel Sumner, Mark Rawlinson and Peter Taylor. He had no sort of social life at all and, to be fair to him, he showed no sign of yearning for one. The school friends he had made in his final year had mostly taken up jobs and had a good deal more money in their pockets than he had. At the same time, few of them would have said that they were doing exactly what they wanted to do for the rest of their lives, and so having a good time at the end of a day's work was important to them.

If Ian envied them in any way he never mentioned it and I do not believe he did feel any pangs of envy. He set himself high standards and a punishing schedule, getting up at 5 a.m. for a training-run, returning to wolf down a quick breakfast before setting off for the practice ground at Denton. There he hit something like 1,000 balls a day and finished it off with putting practice under the lights outside the clubhouse. Often he returned home with his hands bleeding and raw because since he was a small child he had suffered from problems which caused his skin to peel on any part of his body which perspired – notably the gaps between his fingers. To this day he suffers the same chronic problem and cannot wear a golf glove because it induces sweating. When you add to these problems an allergy to a whole variety of things, from grass to cats, it tends to make his choice of profession a trifle strange. Yet he worked at his game through those teenage years with a zeal which bordered upon fanaticism – no discos, no girlfriends, no nights-out-with-the-boys.

For a time I tried to interest him in other things, because both his mother and I felt he was missing out on so much in life which youngsters of his age ought to be enjoying. I almost had to force him to join me on the touchline watching his younger brother playing Rugby with his various XVs as he progressed through Audenshaw Grammar School, but he would spend eighty minutes fretting at this enforced neglect of his Saturday morning practice session. I took him to Manchester's Opera House to see my friends of the D'Oyly Carte Opera Company staging *The Mikado*, but this took him away from his nocturnal putting under the clubhouse lights, and the music was, in any case, substantially less appealing than listening to the Beatles on the transistor radio he could park beside him on the practice ground. It was a strange and lonely adolescence, but Ian never showed the slightest sign of faltering and his parents had to settle for the qualified satisfaction of seeing their first-born doing exactly what he wanted to do every day of his life.

With no really significant sporting traditions in either my family or my wife's, it was a way of life which now intrigued some of our relatives. Indeed, on a visit to Yorkshire my wife was asked by an aunt, 'When is Ian going to get a job?' She replied, 'He has a job – he's learning to be a golfer.' This was clearly an unsatisfactory reply. 'I mean a *proper* job – when will he start earning?' Ah, there we have a good, basic West Riding preoccupation: 'When will he bring home a wage and what will it be?' It was an entirely natural line of inquiry in our family circles and we understood it. What our relatives could not understand was that we were trying to give our son the chance to do what *he* wanted to do with *his* life. It seemed revolutionary and even a trifle mad.

By the end of the summer Ian was a full county player, regularly going off at weekends to play for Lancashire, which I still found rather hard to take. When the dreadful day came for him to turn out against Yorkshire his parents had a long and earnest discussion of what their attitude should be to this fixture. Eventually we decided that while we most earnestly hoped for an overall Yorkshire victory it would be permissible to wish for Ian to win his singles and foursomes. And that's what happened.

Because we could not go to this notable contest ourselves, Ian was picked up by a young, but seasoned, Lancashire campaigner, Alan Squires from Oldham. After that Alan regularly provided transport for his younger team-mate, often travelling miles out of his way to do so. A thoroughly nice man, Alan Squires, and nearly twenty years later he is still one of Lancashire's most distinguished amateur golfers, whose results are read with interest and pleasure by the Mosey family.

In the winter of 1969–70, when Ian was eighteen, we started to think that he ought to be given the chance of practising and

playing during the drearier parts of the English year, somewhere where the weather was a little kinder. Spain was the
obvious place but finance was, as ever, the problem. I was now
a head of department (Outside Broadcasts) at the BBC's North
Regional headquarters in Manchester, but if the salary had
improved from that £1,300 a year starting point expenses had
increased as well, and Ian's younger brother Andrew was now
in grammar school and needing a certain amount of financial
support. It was Ian himself who came up with a bright idea
which seemed to offer a reasonable solution.

Ian: I had met in local golf circles a successful businessman
called Archie Preston at the Dunham Forest Club, near Altrin-
cham, who was also captain at the Atalaya Park Golf and
Country Club near Marbella. Knowing that I wanted to get
away during the winter, he rang me to say that he could fix it so
that I could play through the winter at the club without having
to pay any sort of fees. Better still, his wife wanted someone to
take her Sunbeam Rapier car to Spain so that she could use it
when in residence there. Archie would arrange somewhere for
me to live which wouldn't cost the earth, and altogether it was a
very exciting prospect.

Don: My wife and I were, of course, grateful for Archie
Preston's generous help, but not wildly enthusiastic about
everything that was involved. Ian had been out of Britain just
once, on a family holiday to Spain which had put me, at any
rate, off package-deal breaks for evermore; and in less than a
year since getting his first driving licence he had built up a quite
impressive record of misfortunes. Gate-posts had developed the
habit of leaping out into the road and savaging whatever car he
happened to be driving, or cars in front of him would un-
accountably stop suddenly with unfortunate consequences for
their boot and his bonnet. Mrs Preston's car had a left-hand
drive and this, combined with the fact that Ian would be
driving on the 'wrong' side of the road for the first time, inspired
little parental confidence. Still, we thought, the fledgeling must
fly the nest at some stage, so why not on the Great Adventure?
Off he went to Southampton and a car-ferry to Bilbao.

Ian: It did not take long to learn that I shared my lady
mother's susceptibility to sea sickness. There was, it seemed, a

continuous storm blowing for the whole of the voyage and I spent my time alternately convinced that I was dying or wishing I was dead. By the time we reached Bilbao my taste for adventure had diminished to a marked extent. Enthusiasm was not re-kindled when I realised it had not been the best idea in the world to set out without any maps. Geography had not been my strong suit in an undistinguished academic progress through school, and as I did not speak a single word of Spanish it promised to be slightly tricky finding my way to Madrid – where the car was booked into a train-ferry to take it to Malaga, from where it would be a comfortably short trip to Marbella. I was saved by the fact that most roads in Spain lead ultimately to Madrid, and by placing the sea at my back and heading in the opposite direction (which mercifully was south) I eventually found my way to the Spanish capital.

Here I struck my next major snag. Sitting in Archie Preston's office in Manchester it had all seemed pretty straightforward – I would make my way to the station, present the documents I was carrying with me, have a good rest while the car was being transported through the night and the following day present myself at Atalaya Park. It didn't work out quite like that . . . First of all, I had omitted to check from *which* station trains left for Malaga. On my own in a city the size of Madrid for the first time, I cruised around for hours trying to find the right place. No one – but no one – seemed to speak English, and something of father's deep-seated xenophobia began to develop in my own character in those few hours. Why couldn't someone speak English, damn it? I tried to phone Atalaya Park to report that I was getting a little behind schedule and, you've guessed it, the voice at the other end spoke no English! I was still dressed in the clothes I had worn during my insanitary voyage from Southampton; I had had virtually nothing to eat and I was totally exhausted. The Great Adventure had turned very sour indeed.

After a few hours' sleep in the car I pressed on to drive the whole way and learned something I wish I had picked up at school – there are a lot of high mountains in south-eastern Spain and I now had to drive over the Sierras. The limited amount of driving I had done in England had involved nothing like this, and as I rounded one hairpin bend after another, fear

was now added to the mixed reactions I was already experiencing – hunger, weariness, loneliness and, yes, homesickness.
Even having the old man complaining about some newly
discovered defect in my character was better than this. Somehow I got through the Sierras and finally reached Atalaya Park
only one day later than expected. It seemed a century since I had
left home full of anticipation at the adventures ahead of me.

The next stage of my rude, if gradual, awakening to the harsh
realities of life came when I made my way to the accommodation which had been arranged for me. Archie, true to his
word, had found a place for me and had chosen it on the basis
that I would not have any spare cash for luxuries of any sort. It
was clean, but it was Spartan – the Pensione Gallia. Now, I
suppose very few teenagers of my generation have given much
thought to being brought up in a warm, comfortable and loving
environment. It would probably be an embarrassment to
harbour such thoughts. But it now hit me with shattering force
that life for the next few months was going to be a very different
sort of existence from the only other I had ever known. The
Pensione Gallia was quite simply a workingmen's boarding-
house.

The family and my fellow residents seemed pleasant and
friendly, but I had no means at all of having any conversation
with them. My room with bare, whitewashed walls, was about
seven feet by five feet with absolutely no room at all for anything
except my bed and a small washbasin into which cold water
flowed for about three or four hours a day. I was what is known
as a 'funny eater', meaning quite simply that I was gastronomi-
cally conservative in the extreme, accustomed to mother providing me only with food that I liked and was used to. Any
dislikes I had would now have to be indicated by sign-language;
any preferences I might have as far as diet was concerned would
be irrelevant. I might have driven away from Manchester
feeling something of a man-of-the-world but now the truth hit
me with sickening force: I was an eighteen-year-old teetotal,
non-smoking virgin, away from home for the first time. An
overwhelming sense of loneliness and isolation enveloped me.

The water supply of San Pedro was imperfect in many ways
and even the locals suffered from diarrhoea; there was one small

toilet for each floor of the pensione, for which there was always a queue, and the pervading smell of the establishment each morning was not one of orange groves and sea breezes. Still, for something like 100 pesetas a day (including lunch and evening meal) I could not expect much more and at least it seemed likely that at less than ten bob a day it would help me get through the winter without having to ask the old folks for money too often. Getting used to the food was a more pressing and immediate problem. I was out for lunch (that usually consisted of oranges at the club between practice sessions), and the evening meal followed the same pattern every day: a huge tureen of soup – clear, with either egg or potato added – of which we could eat as much as we liked. It was obviously nutritious but I hated it at first. Amongst the many things I did not eat at home was eggs! As for the main course, paella was the weekly treat, served on Fridays, and my fellow-residents looked forward to this with obvious pleasure. The first I saw was really impressive – a huge pyramid of rice topped by a squid with the tentacles arranged gracefully to drape down the sides of the rice. I shuddered with mingled horror and revulsion while being fascinated by the presentation. On the remaining evenings we often had chips, greasy from being cooked in olive oil and nothing like those I was accustomed to at home. I remember having steak occasionally, cut very thin and again cooked in olive oil, but my mind seems to have shut off the memory of other meals in the Pensione Gallia. That first evening after my arrival I went for a walk around the village, dreading the thought of life in my monastic cell for the next three or four months and wondering if I was ever going to eat a meal again. My prevailing thought was: How can I get out of this?

However, things began to look a little brighter when I went to Atalaya Park (three miles away) the following day. I was half-hoping there might be some sort of job for me there to supplement the money I had brought from home but, while I was disappointed to find there was no work, the golf had been sorted out by Archie Preston and everyone was expecting me. I met the club secretary and the pro, Derek Strachan, who was to become my good friend and to make life very much more bearable. It was a mild, pleasant, Costa del Sol sort of day, and with the palms swaying in the Mediterranean breeze the world seemed a slightly better place I started to come to terms with the Great Adventure.

In all these circumstances, my social life was a bit slow to take off. During the day I could throw myself into working on my game but when the shadows began to lengthen over Atalaya Park there was the problem of what to do with the remaining half of the twenty-four hours. Mercifully, I was befriended by a young assistant manager in Archie's property-development business who spoke English. I am ashamed to say that I cannot remember his name – I wish I could because I remember him with so much gratitude. He sensed at once that I was 'lost' and took me to his home twice a week for dinner. His family were delightful, but spoke no English, and I had not had time to pick up any conversational Spanish. He had, however, a very pretty sister and (without realising the social implications or the cultural differences) I asked her out a couple of times. She came, we went for a walk – and her elder brother came, too! As she was trying to learn English, my first romantic encounters in Spain took the form of halting attempts to communicate with each other with much fractured pronunciation and a good deal of laughter, which at least was therapeutic.

In the golfing sense, Derek Strachan was my saviour. He was roughly the same generation as my teacher at home (Brian Allen) and I like to think he saw in me a genuine desire to improve my game. He gave me some coaching but, being a different type from Brian in that he enjoyed a full social life, and sensing how utterly unworldly I was, he set out to teach me a bit about Life as well. He taught me how to drink, which may or may not have been a good thing, but at least it was useful when he began to introduce me to the cocktail parties for the incoming hordes of wealthy American tourists. As far as they were concerned I appeared to be part of the staff, and so I was asked to play one or two rounds with the visitors and a side-bet enabled me to add a dollar or two to my tiny store of money. Remember, with £3 10s a week I could pay my rent and board at the Pensione Gallia, and I had no other overheads.

It was my friend the assistant manager who helped me break through the egg barrier. At home I not only didn't *eat* eggs, I actually had a phobia about them, convinced I would be sick if I even touched one. So when my friend took me home for Sunday afternoon tea and the opening course was a huge egg salad I took the plunge, closed my eyes and waded through the plateful which was placed before me, waiting for the social disgrace of regurgitation. Nothing happened and thereafter my weekly treat became a visit to the little café in San Pedro for egg and chips, because it was so much less greasy than at the Pensione.

The golf clubs along the coast staged weekly competitions – Wednesday was Atalaya Park, Thursday was Guadalmina, Friday was Nuevo Andalucia – and I worked out a deal with the club secretaries. There was a little trophy of some sort for each competition. (You know what amateur golfers are like – a box of balls doesn't mean anything as a prize but if they can show around a trophy, well that's something different altogether.) So my deal was that if I won a trophy I would sell it back to the secretary for use the following week. I didn't do this with all of them; I brought back seven or eight because I knew my folks would like to put them on show. After playing every day for three months I developed a fair success rate in those competitions. There was virtually no one else out there in my sort of situation so the competition was not too serious.

Later on I met John O'Leary (who had a crewcut at the time, was built like Adonis and hit the ball for miles); also a young man, the son of wealthy parents, who breezed into town and got himself a very nice apartment at the other end of San Pedro. With the help of Derek Strachan, and in the natural process of growing up – my, how I grew up that winter! – I had surrendered my virginal status and when I managed to pull a willing bird I did a swop with this chap, taking over his apartment for the night while he moved into my cell. There had to be a cash adjustment, of course, because he didn't like my place at all but by then I had managed to get together a few pesetas.

The winter passed. When I first set out to drive Mrs Preston's Sunbeam to Atalaya there had been no discussion at home about my return trip. I suppose it was simply taken for granted that if there was a problem at that time the aged parents would solve it somehow. But from the ghastly, empty loneliness of my arrival in San Pedro I remember vividly the night Derek Strachan drove me down the coast to the airport for the flight home. The Sierras show up purple in a certain light and as that was the most perfect evening I was really sorry to leave.

The trip improved my game, even though it is difficult to evaluate to what extent. What it most certainly did do was to help me develop as a person. From the age of fourteen or fifteen, when life for most young people is beginning to pop, I had spent every waking moment on the practice ground or on one golf course or another. My schoolfriends, who had been compelled by circumstances to go into jobs they perhaps didn't really like, compensated by enjoying a fair social whirl. I knew nothing of that. In the Carris Boys' team I was far and away the most unworldly of the whole bunch – streets behind any of them in appreciation of what life is about. Sadly, perhaps, I did not come back with the ability to speak Spanish even remotely well; what I did gain was an extensive vocabulary of nouns, but without any grammar to help me string them together, and that may have been a wasted opportunity. But my priorities were (a) simply to exist in an utterly alien environment and (b) to improve my golf.

One of the highlights of that first winter abroad was to win a pro–am with Ken Bousfield, the former Ryder Cup player, at Atalaya, and to learn that Ken had been reported in a news-paper back home as saying, 'I was most impressed by Ian's golf. He is excellent material and I like his method and swing.' Probably I liked even more the fact that my sweep-winnings in that competition enabled me to buy a reasonable Christmas dinner, but I couldn't help thinking about the dinner my parents and young Andrew would be eating at home!

Don: Letter-writing has never been Ian's strong point and it probably seems quaintly old-fashioned in the late eighties that a couple of parents worried themselves sick about an eighteen-year-old travelling abroad for the first time and sending little or no information back home. But worry we did – terribly. My wife and I were both blessed with deeply caring parents and we hope that is how we have addressed ourselves to our own children. If we had had even a faint inkling of the way he felt in those first days in San Pedro we would have mortgaged the house quite happily to fly out and bring him home. It is difficult to emphasise more vividly than Ian himself has done just how unprepared he was for those four months abroad. But it was the right thing to let him stretch his wings at last.

He came home with the five sub-70 cards he needed to get his scratch rating, a bagful of trophies and a strange new bursting self-confidence. His final letter told us (briefly, as ever) that he had been invited to stay on for the Costa del Sol Championship which ended on 1 March, and asked that he should be entered for the full amateur circuit in 1970, together with as many open tournaments as he might be allowed to enter. I reached for the cheque book. We had lost our little lad for ever, and we now had a massively ambitious golfer on our hands.

Ian: A whole new concept of amateur golf opened up in 1970 when at last I started to mix with the big boys. After getting through two rounds of the British Amateur Championship at Newcastle, County Down, in May, I was swept aside in the third by the redoubtable American, Bill Hyndman. There was a thirty-six-year age difference between us, and that just about paralleled the difference in class, too. I was either two or three under par when I was beaten six and five by the vastly experienced American, who had twice been runner-up in the event. I learned a few lessons on my way round, the greatest perhaps being humility. It had been a good summer in 1969, but this was a very different ball game. Defeats had to be expected more regularly now as I tried my game at an entirely different level; all I could do was watch and learn and practise. In July I went off to Scotland to play two qualifying rounds for the greatest contest of all, the Open Championship. I had £30 in my pocket, (saved by helping with bread deliveries at six in the morning, which left me the remainder of the day to practise) and great hope in my heart.

Don: Ian was entered for everything on the amateur circuit that year. Tony Jacklin's success in The Open Championship the previous summer had fired every Englishman with a greater belief in himself, but we regarded this trip to Scotland as really little more than a chance for the boy to rub shoulders for a couple of days with a lot of professionals and then perhaps watch The Open for a round or two. He was quartered with a friend of mine, Dave Rollo, the Fife farmer who won forty caps in the front row for Scotland and with whom I had toured South Africa, as a newspaperman, ten years earlier. Dave and his wife Jean were (and are) a super couple and I knew they would look after the youngster; indeed they did. They became very fond of Ian, and he of them, and he has often stayed with the Rollos on subsequent visits to Scotland and introduced a number of friends to the farm at Wester Forret, about eight miles from St Andrews.

So off went the boy in my Sunbeam Rapier which – inevitably – came back with a dented wing, the result of one of those hostile gate-posts leaping out from the entrance to the farm and mangling the car without provocation (or so the story went on my son's return). It was difficult to be too angry, however, when he qualified to play in The Open Championship at the world headquarters of the game, St Andrews.

After the first of two pre-qualifying rounds on the Monifieth course, with a 74, his name stood last of the sixty-one listed in our *Daily Telegraph*, so he would have to do something rather good in the second round to have any chance. The eighteen-year-old amateur was lined up in his particular pre-qualifier against seasoned professionals like Vicente Fernandez, Christy O'Connor Jnr, a whole crop of South Africans and New Zealanders plus his teacher, Brian Allen, formerly of Denton. On the first tee he knew he had to shoot no worse than 69 to have any chance – and he did it. At about eight o'clock he telephoned home to announce: 'There are about two hundred pros here, all hating me.' It was a touch of boyish arrogance which I'm sure Ian has remembered on a lot of occasions which followed, when *he* was the one hating a teenage amateur who had got into The Open while he himself failed to do so. But he was understandably cock-a-hoop at the time, and while I spent a good deal of my time in those formative years trying to keep his feet firmly on the ground – there were altogether too many people willing to fawn and flatter and tell him how good he was – I had no thought but to share his delight at that time. Ian spent the next four days in a heady daze of pure joy, playing practice rounds with Peter Alliss and Dave Thomas, standing alongside Gary Player on the practice ground and, indeed, matching Player's 74 in the first round of The Open. And at St Andrews, too. At that time he bore a marked resemblance to Bernard Gallacher, and as he walked round the streets of the wonderful old city he was asked for his autograph every few yards. We have often wondered what the autograph-hunters thought when they had deciphered a rather spidery signature and found it was not Bernard's.

Ian: Since then a lot of tournament rounds have gone into the book. I have played alongside Ballesteros, Lyle, Langer, Norman, Faldo, David Graham and many of the top Americans, but it is difficult to think of any thrill greater than that of teeing off in my first Open in front of the world headquarters of golf, of realising that I was in the same field as Nicklaus, Palmer, Peter Thomson, Doug Sanders and Billy Casper. And along with me were some of my amateur pals, listed in the *Telegraph* as *Mr* Warren Humphreys and *Mr* Nigel Sumner, along with that distinguished golf correspondent, *Mr* D. M. A. Steel. After sixteen years on the tournament circuit I now take a more pragmatic view of playing in The Open but at eighteen, there for the first time, it was the greatest moment of my life – so far.

Don: If it was something of an anti-climax to return to club golf for a day Ian didn't show it when he did a record seven-under-par 65 for the first eighteen at Denton to win the club's thirty-six-hole match-play championship by thirteen and eleven and the following month he teamed up with Kathryn Phillips, the Curtis Cup player from Bradford (the daughter of a friend of mine) to win the Central England Open Mixed Foursomes at Woodhall Spa. It had been a good year.

Ian: During the winter of 1970–1 I got myself some highly unofficial work with a firm of industrial cleaners. In the building trade I would have been part of the Lump, that flying squad of labour who might not have all the necessary documents to satisfy officials of the Ministry of Labour but were ready, willing and able to take on anything at a moment's notice. As the junior member of my fraternity I was naturally given the dirtiest and heaviest duties; cleaning windows at heights which frankly terrified me became one of the more pleasurable tasks. But at least it built up the kitty better than bread deliveries had done, and I started to discover muscles where previously I had not known they existed. With savings of £200 I bought my first car – a twelve-year old banger.

As the new season started, Eddie Birchenough and I won our foursomes in the West Yorkshire *v.* Manchester and District Inter-Alliance Trophy, and then I found myself matched in the top singles with Rodney Foster, a delightfully genial off-the-course companion but very much a Walker Cup player on it. That two and one victory gave me as much pleasure as any I had achieved up to that point; I really felt I had won something worthwhile. Then I teamed up with Ian Gradwell to win the Antlers of Royal Mid-Surrey; on the way home the big end went on my 'new' car. As it had been bought despite the sternest warnings from the old man I feared the worst.

Don: I suppose it is a measure of Ian's expectations of parental wrath that it was young Gradwell who phoned an SOS to *his* home. A telephone call from his father was my first indication that the two youngsters were now stranded at Leicester Forest East service area, which they had reached only after a tow. Gradwell père made the trip down the M1 to bring them home and to resist the efforts of a rapacious mechanic to rip off an exorbitant towing fee.

It did nothing to soften my anger that Mr Gradwell had had to turn out in the late evening to make a round trip of a couple of hundred miles, and my embarrassment at this meant that my son and heir was heading back towards a very large rocket. And then I thought: The poor kid has slogged away for most of the winter doing all the dirty jobs that firm could find for him. The delight of owning one's own first car is something special and he'll be distraught about that. I'd better go easy on him.

Ian: That's not *quite* the way I remember it . . . However, there were considerable complications now because I had to get to Hillside (Southport) to play in the Brabazon and Dad needed his own car. I borrowed Eddie Birchenough's, drove to Hillside and shot a first-round 69. In the *Financial Times*, Ben Wright (now a TV commentator in the USA) reported: 'Mosey is a manufactured golfer, fashioned by a tournament pro-fessional, Brian Allen, now of Stockport. Having put on half a stone during the winter his greater length allowed him to get up at three holes over 500 yards long – he reached the eleventh, measuring 515 yards, with a five-iron.' I wish I could do it now!

Don: The complication arose because, of the two Rugby League commentators we had in the North Region, one was ill and the other not available for the Challenge Cup Final due the following Saturday. As the RL Cup Final was one of my production responsibilities I had to do the commentary myself. However, by going to London by train I was able to let Ian have my car for the following three days. His first-round 69 was a record for the newly lengthened course, but there was a long way to go yet. He reached the final day with probably the world's best amateur at that time, Michael Bonallack, as his playing partner, and this was obviously Ian's most daunting confrontation so far in his golfing life. He missed an eagle three by a whisker on the seventeenth, which would have levelled the scores, and went for a birdie at the last with a daring which he would certainly not be tempted to try in his professional life. It cost him an extra dropped shot and so he finished third behind Scott Macdonald, as well as Bonallack. Pat Ward-Thomas reported in the *Guardian*: 'In the end, massive experience prevailed.' It was Bonallack's fourth Brabazon victory. It brought Ian a non-travelling reserve invitation for the European team championship the following month.

When he was not required in Lausanne he went off to the north-east to win the Ravensworth Open with 68, 67 after a wonderful second-round battle with Gordon Clark, a former British Amateur champion, and then came youth internationals for Great Britain and Ireland *v*. Europe and for England against Scotland. On 30 July the letter we had been aching to see dropped through the letter-box in Denton – Ian's invitation to play for the full England side in the home internationals at Formby. He was paired with Gordon Clark in the foursomes against Wales and they had a comfortable four and two win as England scored a three matches to one win, but in the afternoon it was a rather different story. Playing at the tail of the field against the veteran W. I. Tucker, he was delighted to see his opening tee shot sail more than fifty yards past his opponent's; it was only when he found himself with a long putt to get a half that he suddenly realised there was more to international golf – even against an opponent he regarded, with all the brashness of youth, as 'an old man' – than giving the ball a big whizz off the tee. He lost his singles match against Ireland and did not play in the foursomes; he won the singles and foursomes (again with Clark) against Scotland.

Ian: The 1972 Brabazon caused a few heart flutters when I shot a last-round 69, which equalled the course record at Royal Liverpool (Hoylake). The round started with Peter Moody standing nine shots ahead of me, and after coming home in 33 at least I set a target for Peter. However, he kept splendidly cool in the later stages and finished with six pars to stay one stroke ahead at the end. Well, it was an improvement on the Hillside Brabazon. In July I was delighted to get into The Open again and this time to reach the third round, missing the last day by two strokes but it left me joint leading amateur with Rodney Foster and Sandy Stephen. Next came the leading amateur award in the Benson and Hedges International at York.

Don: In August, Ian captained the England Youth team against Scotland at Glasgow Gailes, an honour which gave my wife and me the most enormous pleasure and pride (although he had flu at the time and his mother felt he ought to be in sick-bed rather than fighting the winds off the Firth of Clyde). The top singles, in which he played Sandy Stephen, was, according to John Campbell in the *Daily Telegraph*, 'A fine game. Birdies were hurled from both sides before Mosey clinched a hard-earned victory on the last green.'

The family album includes a group photograph of that Youth team with so many fine young golfers: Andrew Chandler, Peter Berry, 'Pip' Elson, Howard Clark, Martin Foster, John Putt, Carl Mason, Bob Larratt, Roger Revell, David J. Russell and Ken Saint. Of that smiling band, Howard Clark is undoubtedly the one who has gone on to the greatest success on the tournament circuit, with wins in the Madrid Open (three times), the Portuguese, the Jersey and Glasgow Opens, the Moroccan and PLM Opens and the PGA Championship. He has been a member of three Ryder Cup teams, and figured in the Hennessey Cognac Cup, the World Cup (twice), the Dunhill Cup and the Kirin Cup – a splendid record. But some of the others have built careers, if more modest ones, in the game too.

Ian: The strangest thing to me is that I would have said at the time that Roger Revell was the best player of us all. What happened to him?

Don: Golf had become a more egalitarian game than in pre-war days, certainly at amateur level, but it still had its share of social pitfalls, especially for the band of working-class lads from Yorkshire and Lancashire when they found themselves in some of the more exalted echelons of the game. And in jumping from his winter world of industrial cleaning alongside work-mates whose manners and customs would not really have found favour on a country house weekend, Ian was attempting a social pole-vault of formidable proportions. He had spent months in the company of those honest northern toilers; when April arrived, the environment underwent a marked change. For the Golf Illustrated Gold Vase at Sunningdale, Ian and Andrew Chandler were invited to stay at the home of Gerald Micklem, one of the grand old gentlemen of golf and an administrator of the game of the highest patrician stature. After being knocked out of the competition, the two youngsters were ill-advised enough to spend rather too long in the clubhouse bar in dubious company.

Ian: When the drowning of our sorrows was pretty far advanced, a message arrived from Gerald: 'Tell Mosey that dinner is at seven. I want him there dead or alive, drunk or sober.' Well, at least 'Chubby' and I were on parade on time; I can put it no higher than that. But it was a gesture, well-meaning but utterly misguided, of helpfulness which caused me to die the social death.

It was a fairly formal dinner party, with a number of guests who included Peter Ryde, golf correspondent of *The Times*, no less. I was seated at one corner of the table, which was not the most convenient place for Ellis, the aged family retainer, to serve me. Ellis was straight out of the pages of P. G. Wodehouse, a butler of the old school. In fact I wouldn't be surprised to learn that somewhere amongst the Woosters and the Marriners and the Earls of Blandings there is a character based specifically on the old boy, who seemed to me to be about 120 years old. He was not what you would call a slick mover, and edging round the back of me to complete his serving of the

meal was clearly proving something of a problem. *So I suggested,
all bonhomie and goodwill, that it might be more convenient for him to
serve me from the 'wrong' side.*

What a monumental gaffe that was! Ellis threw a complete
wobbler and spent the remainder of the evening in a state of
severe shock.

If I had not been anaesthetised by my over-long visit to the
bar I might possibly have recognised the enormity of what I
had done. Ellis's sense of outrage at being asked to depart from
the paths of butlering righteousness was manifest throughout
the meal. He actually *sulked* and approached my end of the table
only with the greatest, and most obvious, sense of reluctance. If
he could have dismissed me to the servants' quarters to eat with
the lower orders (which was plainly where he felt I ought to be)
I feel sure he would have done so. From Mr Ryde, on my right,
it was possible to feel high literary disapproval oozing from
every pore. .

I was never invited to stay with Gerald again. I am happy to
report, however, that in purely golfing matters he remained a
good friend, counsellor and supporter.

Don: In August 1972 Ian was twenty-one, and after a
six-year apprenticeship it seemed the right time for him to turn
professional. But after six years of carefully supervising his
amateur career I now made the terrible mistake of allowing –
almost compelling – him to go it alone. It was a time when I
should have sat down and gone through a complete list of the
contacts I had built up in my own working life to see who might
be likely to help with some form of sponsorship. Professional
golf, at any rate on the tournament circuit, was still developing
at a gradual pace; it was not at that time the major television
attraction it is today, and therefore there was not as much
sponsorship money around, either for prize money or for the
backing of hopeful youngsters from the amateur ranks. But the
plain fact is that I did not work anything like hard enough to get
some support for Ian's new venture. Quite simply, I chucked
him in the deep end and left him to find out for himself if he
could keep his head above water; it was a terrible abdication of
paternal responsibility and I left my son with a most desperate
struggle on his hands to make a living. I did not think it through

with the care and concern which was necessary. In a terribly cavalier fashion I left him to fend for himself at the very time when he most needed my help. He has never complained about this. He has never, at any time, said, 'If only we had gone about this another way,' or anything which even remotely implied regret or reproach. In September 1972 he quietly applied for his PGA card and in October he was delighted to win his first prize-money – £5 for finishing joint fourth in a pro–am at Ashton-on-Mersey. There was now a long winter in which to prepare for a whole new way of life. In his full-time amateur years I had written for entry forms for all the tournaments, posted them with the entry fees, kept the diary of engagements and generally looked after the paperwork and the finances. Now, rightly or wrongly, I took the view that he would feel better if he was left to work out the details of his own salvation and to make all his own arrangements. His base remained the family home and the Denton club, although there was no question of a professional attachment there. It was simply his practice ground. He would always have a roof over his head and a bit of home cooking when he wanted it, but for everything else he was now on his own.

The following spring he went out into the professional golf world with little or no capital, carrying his clubs in a 'pencil' bag because there would be no question of employing a caddy, his transport arrangements depending to a large extent on the new friends he could make, his accommodation on the continent in the lap of the gods. That he survived at all now seems something of a miracle and he was not, of course, by any means the only young golfer in this position at that time. If I (and other parents in similar situations) had had even the slightest inkling of what life was going to be like during the next few years I feel pretty sure I would have hauled him off the circuit and directed him to the nearest employment exchange. It was not until we started on this book that I learned what life was *really* like for the young pro starting out in the early seventies.

Ian: Looking back on those early touring days in Europe it seems almost unbelievable that some of us are still in the game and on the circuit. I have no idea how the top players arranged their travel and accommodation at that time. Today, you pick up a phone and speak to one or other of the two specialist firms and a complete package is set up for you. In 1973, when I set out on my tournament professional's career, there was virtually no organisation of any kind. The pre-qualifying rounds for each individual tournament were haunted by a crowd of us who formed a kind of sub-culture of the game. Today, newcomers to the tour seem to arrive, virtually to a man, with new equipment, ample sponsorship, a full package of arrangements for travel and accommodation and a readiness to be upset if the courtesy limousine arrives five minutes late at the hotel to transport them to the course. A mere fifteen or sixteen years ago it was all very, very different.

For my first foray into Europe I had a stake of £200 which I had saved in various ways, no sponsorship, no transport and no back-up organisation. I still lived at the family home in Denton, was fed and watered there, and I suppose there was at the back of my mind the knowledge that if I went seriously adrift, some sort of rescue organisation would swing into action and get me home. But this was *very far* back in the mind; it didn't really come into consideration when I set out in those first few years. It was up to me to work out my own salvation. And so, when Denis Durnian offered me a lift in a car towing a trailer-caravan to the 1973 Madrid, Portuguese and Spanish Open Championships, I was more than delighted to accept. I went to Bolton to meet him and there, sure enough, was a big four-berth caravan and a Vauxhall car to pull it across Western Europe. It did not occur to either of us – or if it did, no mention was made – that there might be difficulties in towing a caravan of that size

behind a Viva with an 1100 c.c. engine. The first indication of
possible problems was when we started to climb over the M62
to Yorkshire (for reasons which I simply can't remember –
perhaps we thought it was the quickest route!) and we had to
get into first gear to make it over the Pennines! Another 2,000
miles of driving stretched ahead.

Stopping only for petrol, and driving in shifts, we reached
Madrid after two days and three nights of non-stop motoring.
Thank goodness, most of France is pretty flat, but a head wind
knocked us down into third gear. The ascent to the middle of
Spain gave us a few more problems but we eventually reached
Madrid in not-too-bad shape – but in the middle of the night.
We made our way to the Puerta de Hierro Club, which is stiff,
formal and autocratic – a massive, palatial mansion with two
golf courses, a polo field and acres of grounds. We found a quiet
corner which seemed an ideal place to park the caravan, and
settled down gratefully to sleep the remainder of the night away
in relative comfort. We were awakened in the grey light of dawn
to find an armed security guard tapping on the side of the
caravan. Since he was carrying a blunderbuss-type gun
apparently left over from the Spanish Civil War, which looked
capable of making quite a mess if discharged, we hurried to give
him our full, if bleary-eyed, attention. And as Denis and I did
not have a lot of Spanish, and the guard spoke no English,
communication at first was just a bit tricky, but we managed to
decipher enough to realise that he thought we were a pair of
gypsies. No one at the club had ever seen anyone turn up in a
dusty carvan with the intention of playing golf at Puerta de
Hierro. Only the aristocratic and wealthy used the club in the
normal course of events, and it was clear that even for a
professional tournament the place was not quite geared up to
the arrival of a couple of grimy kids in a caravan. However, it
worked out well once we had made contact with the secretary,
and we were given a place to site the carvan in the club car park,
which was handy for the practice ground. The locker-rooms
were palatial and the showers magnificent, so our stay there
(though brief – we both missed the cut) was comfortable. Then
it was off to Penina to try to qualify for the Portuguese.

The fact that there are twenty-four hours in a day simply

meant to us that there are twenty-four hours available for
travel. Doing the trip on a shoestring, there was no thought of
staying overnight, even in the caravan; we had just played in
our first professional tournament and now we were anxious to
get to our second in the hope of a better result. We had to
pre-qualify, and therefore the more practice we could get at
Penina, the more chance we might have of lasting the four days
of the Portuguese Open. Armed with an AA road map which we
scrutinised inexpertly, we were unprepared for the geographical obstruction presented by the river Guadiana. Thus, between two and three in the morning we arrived in the border
town of Ayamonte and spotted a sign indicating 'Portugal'. We
followed this until we were confronted by a river which seemed
about a mile wide – and no bridge. This suggested to us that we
had come the wrong way, so we had to turn round – not the
easiest of tasks in limited space with a caravan in tow – and
make our way back to the town centre and to that sign which,
mocking us, told us that Portugal lay in the direction we had
just tried. We spent the remainder of the night driving up and
down the dock area until we learned that passage across the
river was by ferry – and not the sort of ferry which is accustomed to transporting cars and trailers! Somehow we boarded
the ferry, beam on, so that the front of the car and the rear of the
carvan were hanging over the sides. We managed to get across
and eventually reached Penina, where life began to look a little
more pleasant. We were given a convenient place to park and
Denis, being an ex-Merchant Navy man, was a bit better at
improvisation than me. We cooked some baked beans and we
both felt a bit better. Having missed the cut in Madrid, we were
ahead of the main bunch and so able to enjoy the superb
practice facilities of Penina. We hit thousands of balls and got
ourselves into a bit of form. The result was that I finished
thirteenth in my second professional tournament and won
about £200 in Portuguese notes. It's sixteen years ago but I can
remember playing the final round with Brian Huggett and I
was really heading for quite a high finish until I went six-seven
on holes ten and eleven. But I didn't finish as high as thirteenth
for several years after that.

Next came La Manga, and this really was something of an

adventurous trip because of the mountains. I remember arriving in Granada – in the middle of the night, of course – and in looking for a road sign I spotted a light in the sky which I thought was an aircraft. It was, in fact, in a house high up in the Sierra Nevada because the road out of Granada seems to rise vertically for about the first six miles. Somehow the car made it, and *en route* we discovered that there is plenty of snow in April in parts of Spain. At La Manga I started my six-year anti-love affair with the place (before it had been developed): six consecutive Opens and I never made the cut or even threatened to.

Denis in those days was nothing like the accomplished player he has become in the 1980s and, both of us having missed the cut, we set off back home early to get ready for a tournament at Hill Barn, in Worthing. But first the car, having done more for us than we had any right to expect, voiced its final protest in a town somewhere in the south of France. The bit of metal (this may give some indication of our pooled mechanical knowledge) which comes out of the engine block and turns the fan belt sheared off completely. But we were learning to improvise a little more every day.

We unhitched the caravan, drove the car (which would just go for a couple of minutes at a time before it overheated) and after an eternity we tracked down a General Motors dealer who took a piece of an old wreck and welded it on to our engine block. This was some sort of engineering miracle and, we were able after recovering the caravan, to make progress, but it was not an exact fit – so while the fan-belt cooled the system it generated nothing for the battery. We had no electrics for the remainder of the trip across France! But time was pressing. We had to get to Hill Barn and try to pre-qualify, and we had lost twenty-four hours or more getting the emergency repair carried out. Now we travelled north with no power for the cassette-player which had done so much to keep us reasonably sane through the long spells of non-stop driving – but that was the least of our worries. We had no heater, windscreen wiper or lights. And to get to Worthing it was necessary to drive through the night. We got behind a juggernaut and somehow managed to stay there, all night long, with no lights of our own. We were now very tired and, since we were breaking so many laws, we decided that one more breach couldn't really matter, and took turns to rest in the caravan between driving stints.

It was while Denis was sleeping that I got a bit of a sway on the caravan going down a hill and the car hadn't enough power to get us out of it. Mercifully, the hill bottomed out fairly quickly and, as my heart-beat slowly began to return to normal, I noticed a light flashing behind me. It could only be coming from the interior of the caravan because (no proper wing-mirrors!) nothing else was visible to the road. What's the matter with Denis? I thought. The worst is over, now. But when I stopped I realised that the lateral movement of the caravan on the hill had emptied all the drawers and cupboards over the slumbering Durnian. What had been infinitely more alarming was that the calor-gas cylinder had come loose from its moorings, missed Denis's foot by inches and, apart from giving him the fright of his life, had now embedded itself in the side of the caravan. We felt it was time to take a break. By the time we reached home we had cut so many corners, and broken so many motoring regulations, that we were glad of a series of tournaments at home to get our nerve back.

Possibly we might have learned a lesson or two but, if we had, the knowledge would simply be put to use on future sorties abroad. There could be no question of *not* taking chances if one wanted to play the tournament circuit. I had no sponsorship, no backing of any kind outside my family's moral support; I made my way around by any means I could fashion, carrying my clubs in a 'pencil' bag – I never had a caddie until I had been on the circuit for five or six years – and wearing a pair of rubber golf shoes which were hell on the feet but were indestructible. My worldly possessions fitted comfortably into a holdall.

Thus was I equipped when I set out in 1975 to play the Swiss, Swedish, German and Dutch Opens with £40 in my pocket and a one-way ticket to Geneva. I missed the cut at Crans-sur-Sierre, so with £40 less my train-fare from Geneva to Sierre I had now to get to Malmo, Bremen and Hilversum. And to try to win some money. During the Swiss I got into conversation with Simon Cox, who was being sponsored by someone who had provided him with a Leyland Autosleeper, a very swish dormobile. One other guy joined us, with the three of us sharing petrol costs. After some of my excursions, grateful though I was for all lifts, this was luxury travel and we reached Malmo quite painlessly. It was my first visit to Sweden and the story was that all competitors would be accommodated by local people. This was true, but the prospective hosts were expecting golfers of repute to arrive the following week, not three struggling kids turning up on their doorsteps long before the event. The pre-qualifiers were indeed a sub-culture of the circuit. We all knew each other; some of us knew the pre-qualifying courses. We lived a sort of twilight existence in which one could go for weeks without getting as far as the tournament course itself. In our world there were no tournament road signs, no spectators, no prize money – nothing, and sometimes we went weeks without even seeing a PGA official. It was our own little world and, while we were desperate to break out of it, we nevertheless had our own camaraderie, our own *esprit de corps*, very nearly our own code of conduct. There was a great willingness to share bits of good fortune, pieces of helpful information, pointers about friendly and hospitable billets. It was a mad sort of existence in so many ways and yet I wouldn't have missed a day of it for anything.

So here we were in Malmo on Wednesday with nowhere to stay until at least the following Sunday (when the main body of the invading army of golfers began to put in an appearance) and very little money. Eating was not high on our list of priorities, but practice was. So, once again, we hit thousands of balls while waiting for the pre-qualifying rounds. By Sunday I moved in with a smashing Swedish family. My host ran a small engineering company with excellent recreational facilities for his employees – including a jacuzzi – so, for my fellow-boarder, Ian Wrigley, and myself, there were a couple of days of luxury. I failed to pre-qualify. Next stop, Bremen.

It was Simon Cox, bless him, to the rescue again to get across to Germany and I loved the course. I would dearly have liked to play in the tournament proper for obvious reasons, but also because I enjoyed the course so much. Instead, I played the pre-qualifying round on the tournament course – and failed to qualify by miles. I shot eighty-plenty and moved on to Holland. The Bremen week had not been memorable in any way but the following week was.

I now ran into Gary Birch, another of this shadowy world of
pre-qualifiers who roamed Europe, really not a part of the
tournament circuit at all, but reminiscent, I suppose, of the
roving bands of mercenaries who wandered about Europe
in the Middle Ages, hoping to be employed by some local
condottieri. In our case, our hopes were aimed no higher than
getting through a pre-qualifying round and returning later to
the sub-culture, where any story of taking part in a real
tournament was listened to with avid attention. That was the
other world, the world we somehow (without really knowing
how) hoped to reach in due course. Gary was a splendid eccentric. I had met him a year earlier on a pro–am (literally) flying visit to Florida and some time after that he had asked me, on
the basis of a very sketchy acquaintance, it seemed, to be his best
man. The wedding had taken place just before this European
leg of the circuit had started, and Gary was now taking his bride
on a slightly delayed honeymoon – to the Dutch Open Golf
Championship. And they were living in a tent. It was an unbelievably hot summer and around Hilversum it was hotter than
in most other places, so perhaps a tent wasn't such a bad idea, all
other things being equal. But on this particular honeymoon
they were *not* particularly equal because the newly-weds had a
lodger sleeping on the fly-sheet under the awning of their tent. Me.
I had spent a little of what remained from my £40 on a couple
of nights in a Bremen hotel because there was no hospitality
provided there. But I knew we would would be all right in
Holland – the Dutch people were always superb in their hospitality and accommodation was always made available to us.
But not from the previous Monday, nine days before the Open
was due to begin. 'Come back next Sunday,' was the word, 'and
there will be accommodation available for you.' There was not
much money left in the kitty but Gary Birch came to the rescue. So the remainder of the week was spent just the thickness
of a canvas wall away from the consummation of the Birch mar-
riage. Well, I had been their best man, after all . . . G. Birch
figures very high on my list of good-news people of the sub-culture.
At the end of the week I moved into digs at last and found
myself accommodated with Warren Humphreys in the home of
a lady doctor, a member of the Hilversum club. She explained

that she had a busy practice and could not, to her great regret, ferry us to and from the course, which was quite a distance away. But she had an idea: there were a couple of bicycles in the garage and if we didn't mind riding them it might be a way round the problem. We didn't mind at all. Holland is beautifully flat and I had ridden a bike for most of my life, so Humph and I changed into shorts for the ride, back into more formal dress for our practice and stored our gear in the bag-room at the club. And with time to kill, once again we now hit *millions* of balls on the practice ground and enjoyed our days in the sun. Sod's Law then decreed that I got through the pre-qualifying round and at last I was in a tournament-proper. Now if there had been one to miss, for preference, this would have been it. I was going home that week, my £40 after nearly a month away had dwindled almost to nothing and I was looking forward to a bit of mum's cooking. But I made it into the Dutch Open – not without a few problems.

My partners for the pre-qualifying round were Warren and Gary Koch, the American who has since done very well in the USA, and I started eight-seven. This was after I had been on the continent for a month and had not struck one tournament golf ball. I was doomed. Then I played the last sixteen holes in four under par to get one of the last qualifying places by the skin of my teeth. I had an early start in the first round, completed it and promptly behaved like a daft kid again. The son of my hostess invited me to go to a local water-sports centre, where I not only got sunburned but tried water-skiing for the first time. To this day I have never travelled more than three feet above the water-line when water-skiing, and on this first occasion I was quite uniquely inept. Yet in a masochistic sort of way I enjoyed being dragged round under water for something like two hours – my young tutor was exceedingly patient – but the extensive use of the forearms was not really the ideal preparation for the following day's second round of golf. I turned up for it with my arms about a foot longer than they had been in the first round and I missed the cut. It had not been a spectacularly successful venture into Europe.

Every April that cheerful band of nomads who made up the sub-culture started the new circuit with no money at all other than what they had managed to cobble together during the

winter months. We were not exactly the sort of material that
employers were looking for in filling well-paid positions for
three or four months; all we really wanted to do was play golf
and anything else was a means to that end. So when April came
round we were all looking for the cheapest way of doing the first,
contintental, leg of the European tour (or the European pre-
qualifying tour, as it was to most of us). We were now into the
later 1970s; I was a slightly better player than when I had
turned pro but I still had to pre-qualify for everything. Looking
at the five-week duration of that first leg – the Spanish,
Portuguese, Madrid, Italian and French Opens – I just could
not visualise it as a viable venture. I studied it from all angles
and there was just no way that it could be made financially
possible. Nevertheless, a group of us, including Warren
Humphreys and Andrew Chandler, sat down and tried to find a
way to *make* it work.

We had a contact, Frank Braynor, who became something of
a legend in the travel business. He was a great character,
completely mad, who didn't have an agency; he didn't even
have an office. He occupied a corner of someone else's office and
somehow, if he could get his money in quickly enough and pay
his outgoings in the nick of time, he contrived to exist on about a
2 per cent margin. But he could always offer you a cheap deal,
no matter where you wanted to go. He was one of the great
pioneers of the travel agency business, Frank. We'll come back
to him in a minute. First, however, Andrew ('Chubby') Chandler learned of a ticket which took one from Manchester to
Malaga with an option of a stopover in Madrid on the return
leg. And there was no time limit for that return leg; it was an
'open' return and it was so cheap that it opened up the
possibility of hiring a car in Spain. So we worked out that if four
of us bought these cheapie tickets to Malaga, we could hire two
cars to drive to Vilamoura for the Portuguese Open, then drive
back to play Torrequebrada (the Spanish Open), after which
we returned the hire car. But on what seemed to us to be the
Rolls-Royce of air tickets we still had the chance to go on and
play in the Madrid Open. Before we go any further it is
necessary to explain that a change in the pre-qualifying system
had taken place since my interesting journey round Switzer-

land, Sweden, Germany and Holland. If one made the cut and played in the last round of one of these tournaments, it now gave automatic entry to the next one. So, if we reached the final stages of the Portuguese we had no need to pre-qualify for the Spanish, and so on.

We booked our super-cheapie through Frank Braynor, paid him in advance and presented ourselves at Heathrow for our late-night flight to Malaga. No tickets! They were supposed to have been left for us at the Iberian Airlines ticket desk, where no one knew anything about them. We didn't panic easily in those days. I suppose we had become too used to such vicissitudes to get unduly excited until the plane was actually taxi-ing out to the runway without us. One of our number knew someone who had a friend who had a business contact who *might* know where Frank could be found. We tracked him down in due course; he made a series of phone calls (because, of course, cheap as our super-cheapie ticket was, Frank had done a deal of some kind to give him his 2 per cent) and the tickets finally materialised. If the plane was not actually taxi-ing by this time, the doors were certainly about to close. It was ultra-ultra-last-minute and we *almost* reached the panic stage because a highly-elaborate chain of events hung upon our reaching Malaga on that flight.

At Malaga airport, no one knew anything about the hire-cars! No one had even remotely heard of a booking for two small cars for four weary golfers. I rang my girlfriend Mandy (later my wife) in Manchester and got her out of bed; she rang Frank Braynor and got *him* out of bed; he rang someone who rang someone else in Malaga – two other nocturnal upheavals – and ultimately a Spaniard appeared who was not the car-hire man but knew the one who was! Well, it seemed that a fair cross-section of the population of western Europe had now been awakened in the course of that night so what was one more? We knocked up the car-hire man at his home. And in the end we got our cars. We had not yet even started to think about playing golf. In fact we had to drive to another country before we could do that. After two uneasy hours on the phone at Heathrow we had now had three even more uneasy hours in and around Malaga Airport, which, in the absence of the usual Spanish air-traffic-controllers' strike, was deserted apart from one mildly curious security guard. But sheer persistence won the day (or rather the night) and off we went to the Algarve.

I pre-qualified for the Open, dribbled away in the last round to finish something like sixty-fifth, but at least I was now automatically in the Spanish. The Torrequebrada course is interesting and I like it. I had my first glimpse of Bernard Langer, shot twenty-one birdies but a lot of rubbish as well, and finished with a 76 and well down – but I was still exempt for the Madrid Open next week. Now came a bit of a dilemma. I had told Mandy that I was only going to be away for a couple of weeks, and I was not twenty-one more, not so durable. I was feeling the need to get back home for a bit of creature comfort. Yet what was the point of qualifying for the Madrid if I didn't take up the option? The magic ticket would still take me back to England if I did no good at Puerta de Huerra, so off I went to play there. I *just* made the cut and telephoned Mandy to ask her to come down for the weekend. We had a lovely couple of days; I was now pre-qualified for the Italian Open and decided to go on there, but then, on the last day of the Madrid, Mandy's bag (which had been left with my gear in the locker-room) was ripped open and every penny the two of us jointly possessed was stolen.

I was first out in the final round, playing with Nigel Blenkharn, who was to earn my undying gratitude and respect in the next thirty-six hours. Apart from an exemption into the Italian Open, my clubs and a spare shirt or two, I had nothing – no money, no transport, no means of getting Mandy to the airport, no means of getting myself to Monticello – nothing. In the course of that round, Nigel mentioned that he was driving to the Italian but that his car was full. However – what a man! – he said that if I was *completely* stuck he would contrive something. We finished the round about midday and my first problem was to get Mandy on her way back home. She had come out on a one-week charter ticket and the return part was not valid for a flight that day (I sometimes look back and marvel at the situations I created for myself), so we had to spin a yarn about it being vital for her to return home because of a family illness. It was far from easy but somehow we talked her on to the plane and now all I had to worry about was playing two more tournaments in Italy and France without a penny in my pocket, and no transport home to England at the end of them.

The splendid Nigel Blenkharn had hung about waiting for us to sort out Mandy's return home; we now retraced our steps to the golf course and loaded up the car with Nigel, Jeff Hall, 'Prof' Davidson and myself plus luggage plus golf clubs. 'Prof' is a company director who gave up the world of commerce to follow the golf tour as a caddie. He can do the *Times* crossword puzzle in about ten seconds but has difficulty in tying his shoe-laces – in short he's a bit of a character. He has been everywhere and done everything, according to his own CV, and while it does not always turn out to be true (his 'fluent French', for instance, would have been no less incomprehensible in Patagonia than it was at the frontier on that trip) he can be an entertaining travelling-companion. But we run ahead of ourselves.

For the Prof and myself in the back seat the journey was going to be rather like that of astronauts in a space capsule. We were installed first and the bags and the clubs were then stacked around us. Nigel Blenkharn now had to drive right into the centre of Madrid to a street off the Plaza España, where the rush hour lasts from dawn to dusk. This was because Jeff Hall had been staying with his Spanish wife's parents and had kept most of his gear there. So it was already becoming a very long day for Nigel by the time he had threaded his way through the horrendous traffic and out again from the centre of Madrid. It took forever. And once we were clear of the capital and on the road north I breathed a sigh of relief. Mandy was safely on her way home, I had borrowed a bit of money, I was on my way to Italy and I was automatically qualified to play in the Open there. It all looked great.

We had travelled about 150 miles when Jeff Hall said, 'You can just drop me here. I know what you're going to say. It's OK. I can't believe I've done this – *I've left my passport in Madrid.*' I shall admire Nigel Blenkharn for his reception of this news for as long as I live. He never batted an eyelid. I swear it. He just gently brought the car to a halt, turned round and drove back to Madrid.

Once more we threaded our way through the maelstrom of traffic; it was now late at night but the centre of Madrid was still heaving. Jeff ran in to collect his passport; Nigel stepped out to stretch his legs and found that in the last few yards we had run over a nail, or a piece of glass or something of the sort. We had a flat tyre. It was on the off-side, too. We were already parked illegally on a triple yellow line; six lanes of traffic were screaming past, all of it on the side where we had to change the wheel. We had to take everything out of the car to get to the spare wheel as a torrent of cars and taxis and lorries whizzed past us. Even the pavements were blocked solid with pedestrians. It was all unbelievably messy. And still Nigel uttered no word of complaint or reproach. Once again, he never batted an eyelid. I don't think I have ever admired a fellow human being as much as I admired Nigel Blenkharn in that moment.

The spare must have been a bit dodgy because we started with a slow puncture on our way to Italy and graduated to blow-outs and puncture repairs on the trip. It took a long time, about twenty-six hours, before we finally reached Monticello, and if Nigel reflected upon the painless trip he might have had if he had simply driven off from Puerta de Huerra when he had completed his final round the previous day he never, by so much as a word or gesture, gave the slightest indication of it.

I made the cut in the Italian and so was qualified for the French, and I had an interesting round with Langer. Torrequebrada had given me my first glimpse of the German but now I saw him at close quarters. He really could play – he had the big game with all the shots – but he was still at that time a yipper. He just couldn't putt at all, but it was easy enough to see that if he ever overcame that he would be a really great player. He had a fantastic temperament; he would play alongside guys he could *out*play completely, but he just couldn't score. Yet he was very obviously a potential winner. From Monticello. I got a lift to Lyons, for the French, with Ian Woosnam, at that time a complete struggler like the rest of us. He was a good lad, well liked, but he was a part of the sub-culture for years until he came good in the eighties.

From Lyons I got a lift home with Denis Durnian and his new wife and returned to Manchester not much richer in terms of cash but infinitely so in experience. Once again, it had been an eventful tour.

The Eccentrics

Don: It's about time we heard from the splendidly eccentric Gary Birch again, isn't it? There was a story which went the rounds about him trying to play tournament golf with a set of rubber-shafted clubs, or something of the sort, I believe?

Ian: Ah yes. This was in the mid-seventies when a set of clubs called EZ-Swing was on show at the PGA Convention at The Belfry before the tournament season began. They were good-looking clubs, with good heads – until you picked them up and felt the compound material of the shafts wobble about. The idea was to use them as a swing-aid; if you tried to hit the ball with an orthodox stroke you were in danger of decapitating yourself, literally, because the head took such a long time to come through owing to the soft nature of the shaft. It was rather like playing with a hosepipe – the whole club could be bent into a U shape. But they caused quite a bit of interest at the convention because they were used for a long-driving contest and a lot of amusement was caused when the big hitters tried to give it the usual whizz. I suppose a few sets were sold for use as a swing-aid.

Now, the tour began that year in Madrid, went on to Rome and then into France, and there was quite a lot of driving to be done. Gary duly arrived in Madrid towing a large, four-berth caravan behind an under-powered Simca. He had no co-driver so it was going to be a bit of a tiring trip for him; his wife was at home awaiting the birth of their first child, which was imminent; and Gary had brought along a full set of these EZ-Swing clubs to try to pre-qualify, without any back-up set of conventional clubs! Now if I say that off a tee-peg, with your very best swing and a bit of experience, you could just about play with one, that would be it. But I would have liked to see anyone try to play from a buried lie in a bunker. And Gary had the full set, sand iron and all, except the putter. (We felt it showed a certain lack of commitment to use an orthodox putter!) His attempt to pre-qualify in Madrid saw him shoot an 88, which I suppose was a reasonable score using those clubs but it didn't get him into the Madrid Open! And he didn't make it in Italy or France either, so he drove home, still towing the heavyweight caravan behind the light car, to find compensation in the fact that he was now a father.

Don: Golf is a pretty serious and down-to-earth business when you are playing it for a living, and yet Gary Birch was not the only eccentric on the circuit by any means, was he?

Ian: Indeed, no. Some of us remember Danny Goodman with great affection, for instance. He wasn't the most accomplished of players but he absolutely loved his golf. It was his ambition to lay on a huge, big-money tournament for all the pre-qualifiers who were his contemporaries. Anyone who had achieved any sort of success would be barred and the members of the sub-culture would have the field to themselves. Sadly, there were all sorts of practical problems in setting up such a tournament and so it never got off the ground, but it would certainly have been a popular contest. Everyone who ever played with Danny brought back some sort of contribution to the folklore of the game. John Bland, for instance, partnered him in Paris when Danny was having a bad day and was startled to find him sauntering down the side of a fairway accompanying himself on the harmonica in a Bob Dylan number – a snatch of lyrics, a few bars of accompaniment – not *really* the sort of stuff you expect to encounter from a competitor in the middle of the French Open.

During the same tournament, Danny had another bad round, and when the players' coach arrived to take them from the course back to the hotel they threw their clubs into the luggage-hold and climbed aboard. Not so Danny. He put his clubs in with the others, then climbed in after them. No one seems to have noticed, but half way back to the hotel a frenzied hammering was heard from the underside of the coach. The driver stopped, searched for the source of the noise and found Danny in extremis from carbon monoxide fumes amongst the bags of clubs. During a German Open he suffered once again and decided to punish his clubs. He put them down behind the back wheels of his car, solemnly reversed over them and then, to make sure they remembered their transgressions, drove forward over them to give them a second lesson. I always felt that showed a little more style and imagination than simply throwing the bag into a lake.

Danny, as might have been expected, bowed out of the tournament circuit in the grand manner. He was playing in the Portuguese Open at Troia, which is a really tough course. At the short fifth – about a seven- or eight-iron to a postage-stamp green with a deep bunker on one side and the beach on the other – he put his tee-shot into the trap. He thinned his next out of the deep bunker across the green into another bunker on the beach side from where he put it back into the first trap. In utter frustration, Danny changed his club, fired the ball 100 yards on to the beach and he and his caddy just kept walking, off the course and out of tournament golf. It was the last one of the 1983 season and I don't think he has been seen on the circuit since that time. Danny was really born a little later than he should have been. He had a lovely, laid-back personality which really qualified him to be a 1960s hippy with the sort of mid-Atlantic accent and terminology to match. He had a remarkable idiosyncratic swing with an exaggerated bend of the knees which indicated all too clearly that he was never going to make it, but he loved the game, and the life, so much that no one had the heart to tell him. I remember once breakfasting with Danny during the Scandinavian Open when he had failed to qualify for the umpteenth time (like many of us) and he looked at me and asked, 'When is my career going to blossom?' There was as much pathos in the question as any I have ever heard because he really meant it. He absolutely loved tournament golf.

Don: What about your adventures with Andrew Chandler et al?

Ian: A quartet of us, in 1975, worked out that four guys with two cars provided a convenient way of tackling a series of European tournaments since it gave more options in the event of some pre-qualifying for tournaments while others didn't. It might at least save some of us hanging about for several wasted days. Andrew Chandler and I took one car, Howard Clark and

Martin Foster the other and when we reached Madrid, Howard
and Andrew were despatched in search of cheap digs while the
other two lined up facilities at the course where we were to play.
The accommodation-hunters returned with a report: 'We've
found something, but don't expect too much. It's not very
good.' That, as ever, turned out to be a massive understate-
ment. I was the last to arrive and so drew the short straw,
ending up in a room which has gone prominently into the
folklore of the tournament circuit as 'the worst room on the
tour'.

It was in a pensione, right in the middle of Madrid. It was a
miracle that we ever found it, and in fact it had only been
identified by a small plaque on the wall with a single star on it.
A one-star pensione! We should have known what to expect.
The building was of traditional Spanish style – the entrance
through a massive, castle-like door led to a courtyard from
which we ascended five flights of stairs in pitch darkness. The
four of us were quartered in a sort of family apartment, with a
communal dining-area and a lounge which was little more than
a corridor with a couple of seats in it. The bedrooms were off
this corridor and the last one – mine – was just an alcove which
had been partitioned off, so it had no windows. The only way in
which it could have been made more inhospitable than it was in
its natural state was to furnish it as the owners had done. They
had put up shelves which were cluttered with bric-à-brac of a
very strange nature indeed. Perhaps the owners were involved
with the occult in some way. Anyway, their collection of
souvenirs, my poor cell's only ornamentation, appeared to my
over-active imagination to have been collected from a touring
production of Macbeth: 'Eye of newt and toe of frog, wool of bat
and tongue of dog, Adder's fork and blindworm's sting, lizard's
leg and howlet's wing.' They were all there on the shelves. Even
allowing for the stifling, airless claustrophobia of the place,
there was no way I was going to be able to sleep with that stuff
around me.

As a child, I had my share of nightmares and this was like one
of them. I tried to sleep with the light on, but this merely served
to draw my attention to the ghoulish collection which crowded
in on me. Martin Foster shared my horror of the grisly and,

although he was not required to sleep in that atmosphere, the mere consciousness that it existed next door was enough to keep *him* awake, so on the second night we played Scrabble while flattening a bottle of cheap Spanish brandy, real firewater, so that we could render ourselves insensible. It didn't help our fitness for golf but at least we got some sleep.

Don: Didn't you wonder at times whether it was all worth while – the endless pursuit of enough money to take you on to the next tournament, sleeping rough, wondering whether you could afford a meal, dreading another mechanical breakdown? And there could have been few hopes of actually winning a tournament when you had, first, to pre-qualify, then to make the halfway cut, then the second cut, and even when you eventually reached the last day you were not always certain of making a few bob in prize money?

Ian: Not for quite a long time. We were all pretty young and there was a rather wonderful sense of comradeship and a tremendous sense of adventure. No one really knew what next week might bring; the only certainty was that it would bring a new series of hair-raising experiences to some of the sub-culture. Some would be the result of misfortune, some would be caused by lack of foresight, some by sheer incompetence and stupidity. One way and another, it would lead to a swopping of yarns when we got to the next port of call and I suppose in a way it made us all feel a little bit better in the sense of 'a trouble shared'.

Don: So the essential qualities for your group were resilience, adaptability, optimism and a fair amount of cheek?

Ian: That just about sums it up – especially the cheek. Towards the end of the seventies, when neither of us had made much money for a long time, Warren Humphreys and I set off for the German Open in Düsseldorf in his mother's Morris Minor 1000. Our essentially vague plan of campaign was to call upon a cousin of Warren's who was married to an army officer stationed somewhere north-east of Düsseldorf, and hope we would be offered accommodation. We didn't contact her in advance, probably because we feared we might get a polite refusal. I didn't even know how long it was since Warren had seen his cousin and he didn't say. It was essentially a tenuous operation, as most of them were, but with the pre-qualifying round on Monday it gave us enough time to improvise something else if this ploy failed. We set out hoping it *wouldn't* fail but it was all very vague and hit-and-miss. Anyway, we drove first to the course in Düsseldorf to get our bearings, then set off to find the army camp where Warren's cousin-in-law was stationed.

It was about an hour's drive from Düsseldorf, so it was convenient in terms of commuting to the course and all seemed to be going well. The camp was entirely different from what we had expected – nothing like the Victorian barracks which are army billets back in England. We really seemed to be in a few square miles of England on German soil, with a cinema, a fish-and-chip shop, a cricket ground and a shopping centre. We immediately felt that if there was any way we could stay here it would be a very good thing indeed. However, having asked our way to the relatives' quarters we found no one at home, so we were left to drive around for a time during which it emerged that Warren had not seen his cousin since a family wedding several years before and really had had no contact with her at all. At the same time, the more we saw of the camp, the more we liked the idea of billeting ourselves there if it was at all possible.

When the family finally returned home they welcomed us but it soon became clear that with two children in purpose-built army married quarters there was no room for a couple of itinerant golfers. It was now time for us to be very cheeky indeed, but I regret to say that the first thing you learned on the circuit in those days was to be thick-skinned. So we stayed, and we stayed. The welcoming cup of tea had long since been consumed and Warren had run out of family topics of the 'How is Uncle Jim?' type. The husband didn't know either of us and there was no reason in the world for him to feel like putting down the 'Welcome' mat. So we just brazenly sat it out until the question had to be asked, 'Where are you staying?' 'Well, we haven't fixed anywhere yet. Do you know a decent, cheap hotel . . . ?' The children were moved in with mother and father and the long-lost cousin and his friend stayed in their room.

From this unpromising beginning, the relationship improved tremendously. Cousin-in-law gave us a conducted tour of the local pubs and we all got along well. Warren and I both missed the cut but stayed until the weekend, and I think it turned out to be a mutually pleasant experience. I hope so because they were delightful people. So much for cheek; now we move on to incompetence, as the two of us set off to try to pre-qualify in Holland.

During the tournament in Düsseldorf the story had spread through the ranks of the pre-qualifiers that, for the Dutch Open, pre-qualifying day was to be Tuesday and not, as usual, Monday. No one afterwards knew exactly how the rumour started, but by general consent it was accepted and no one bothered to check it! Warren and I took off for Hilversum on the Monday morning in a contented state of mind, despite missing the cut – we were accustomed to such disappointments by this time. We had really enjoyed our stay with his relatives. We were both heavily into physical fitness at the time and early-morning jogging in the woods behind their home had been a great pleasure on the thick carpet of pine needles. The world seemed quite a pleasant place as the Morris Minor 1000 cruised serenely along towards the border. In fact the car was running so well that I was moved to comment to Warren: 'These are great little cars, aren't they. *My* mother has had a couple – it would have been just one if I hadn't pranged the first one – and she has never had a moment's trouble with the engine in either. There is only one snag with them: there's some kind of weakness in the front wheel mounting and occasionally a wheel falls off.'

That fragment of conversation has no immediate relevance, but keep it in mind . . .

As we stopped for a morning break in a small Dutch town I glanced at a clock in the main square and noticed, to my surprise, that it was an hour different from the time indicated on my watch, which I was quite sure was adjusted to European time. I got out the paperwork to see if it indicated the address of the Hilversum course, so we could head directly for it, and that represented the total extent of our joint pre-planning for the Dutch Open Championship. The paperwork then told me that the pre-qualifying round was, contrary to the Düsseldorf

rumour, indeed on Monday; it also told me that the championship was not at Hilversum at all but at Zandvoort, away
on the North Sea coast; and it was at this doom-laden moment
that we discovered we were on the wrong road in any case and
heading for Utrecht rather than Hilversum! On this pleasant,
sunny morning when it seemed that God was very much in his
heaven and all was so completely right with our world we were
in fact *in* the wrong place, *heading* for the wrong place, on the
wrong day and with our watches showing the wrong time.

How incompetent can you get? Believe me, there is no limit to
it. And yet the Divine Providence which hovered benevolently
over us so often in those days did not desert us now. We hared
across the country to Zandvoort, arriving hopelessly late about
three o'clock, to find that so many others had fallen victim to
the Düsseldorf rumour that the PGA, in an unprecedented
move, had waived all the normal conditions and we were now
allowed to play at the end of the field. I went out in par but
Warren, playing dreadfully, shot 42 or 43 for the first nine and
was clearly going to fail to pre-qualify. Self-preservation as
much as personal friendship now prompted me to egg Warren
on through the back nine. If he did not qualify he would not be
given accommodation for the tournament-proper and would
have to drive home; if that happened, I would be left in Holland
without any way of getting home. I virtually browbeat Warren
into playing better on the second nine and he came back in
one-under. Coming up the last we found the green surrounded
by all the hopefuls because our scores would govern what the
pre-qualifying score would be, so everyone had a vested
interest. Warren had to get down with a chip and a putt, which
he did, so we both were now in the Dutch Open.

We were accommodated with a marvellous couple, Tom and
Kristin Sorko, who were both lawyers and two of the most
delightful people I have met anywhere on the circuit. Warren,
from that terrible start, won his biggest cheque of the season for
a finish about seventeenth, but Fate had not finished with us
yet. In one round I had a very early start, so for the only time
during that fortnight in Europe I drove the Minor 1000 while
Kristin brought Warren to the course later. Halfway up the
drive to the golf course, one of the front wheels of the car fell off!

What had I said on the road from Düsseldorf . . . ? Providence now appeared jointly in the guise of the Sorkos, who knew a man who bought up army surplus vehicles and cannibalised them for parts. By some sort of miracle he was currently in possession of a number of Minor 1000s and he was able to tow away our crippled Morris and restore it to a roadworthy condition. It was amazing how frequently someone came to our rescue when all seemed lost.

Don: You've had other notable breakdowns, haven't you?

Ian: Yes, indeed. Doing the Penina–La Manga–Madrid triangle with Noel Hunt in a two-litre Cortina, we experienced a shattered windscreen when we were somewhere near Badajos in the middle of the night with, consequently, no hope of a replacement, and I had my first experience of driving for about six hours with no glass in the front of the car. It is not pleasant, but it is manageable if you can avoid the flying fragments of glass which you thought you had cleared out of framework. On arrival in Penina our angel of mercy on this occasion was the wife of Peter McGuinness (then the pro at Vale do Lobo; whom we had both known in Manchester). Pete was away but his delightful wife took us in, fed and watered us, rang up the local Mr Fixit and in no time at all we had a new windscreen. I made the cut, got to the last day but missed the money, and so we moved on to La Manga, where I *never* did any good, and from there to Club de Campo, in Madrid. By this time Noel, who was newly married, and I (courting strongly) were both thoroughly homesick and disillusioned by our lack of success, so, after reaching the last round but still making no money, we decided to make a bolt for home. Once again we did everything wrong.

It was a weekend, so there were no banks open. We called at one of Madrid's most palatial hotels to change some travellers' cheques and got a really bad rate of exchange, but just enough to buy the petrol which would get us home. We stopped to fill up at a garage just out of town and divided our labour, with me filling up the fuel tank and Noel checking the oil and water. I should have known better than to let him go under the bonnet. Noel (who now runs a hugely successful golfing entertainment of trick shot demonstrations) was renowned on the circuit as an absent-minded-professor type. Every club in Europe must, at some time, have acquired a memento of his visit in the form of at least one article of equipment that he left behind. Now, if you haven't already guessed it, he forgot to replace the oil filler-cap.

Happy and excited to be on the way home, we sped northwards, intent on completing the trip in one dash. All went well – God knows how or why – until we reached the foothills of the Pyrenees and, as we turned into a filling station, the engine died on us. Peering fearfully under the bonnet we found oil everywhere including, of course, on the plugs. No way would the engine start again.

After the usual pantomime of sign language, arm-waving and bellowed nouns (usually with a question mark after them!) we learned that there was a garage a little further along the road, but that it was uphill all the way. This time Providence came mob-handed – a group of youngsters starting a night out, who obligingly gave us a push over the brow of the hill, which was quite a distance away, from where we coasted down to the garage. Late on Sunday night the proprietor was entirely disinclined to start sorting out the follies of two bad drivers. We would have to wait until the morrow. By now it was distinctly chilly in the hills and, as usual, we had no money for a hotel room even if one had been available. So we wrapped ourselves in the warmest clothes we could find and spent an exceedingly uncomfortable night in the car. In the morning the garage boss had a lot of work to do on the cars of more regular clients than us, and so our problems had a very low priority indeed. From his assistant we borrowed a spanner to remove the plugs, wiped them clean and laid them out to dry in the Pyrenean sunshine. We reached Manchester without any further disaster.

Don: This all sounds very much as though you were a jinx, that catastrophe automatically descended upon anyone with whom you travelled. Hadn't you by now got a reputation for being a complete Jonah?

Ian: Far from it. Certainly I was involved in my share of calamities, but amongst the sub-culture such experiences were commonplace. The list is endless, but let's look at just a few of them.

Warren Humphreys, Roddy Carr and Des Smyth set off one year for Spain in a small Datsun with a roof-rack. Somewhere beyond Biarritz, where it is straightforward if you keep to the coast-road, they took a wrong turning and went too far to the east. It was that eerie time of twilight when the light just begins to go and driving can often be trickier than in full darkness with the headlights on. As twilight turned to darkness they found themselves climbing far higher than they should have been and the fuel gauge was flickering perilously close to the 'empty' mark. Now, the philosophy on such occasions is quite simple: 'There must be a filling station just round the next corner. We haven't passed one for miles so there is no point in turning back.' So the three of them drove onwards and upwards. Still no sign of a petrol-station, and now they had to be down to their last thimbleful; the gauge had been reading 'empty' for ten miles or more. It was pitch black and it had started to snow. The realisation began to dawn on them that they could grind to a halt on the top of a mountain in a snowstorm. Words like 'hypothermia' and 'exposure' flickered across their minds; they waited for the car to splutter to its final halt. And then, out of the darkness, a policeman flagged them down: the road ahead had been closed by a landslip, a lorry had gone over the side and was halfway down a ravine; they were stranded.

Now, most motorists will be able to identify with the state of mind of the trio – they knew with absolute certainty that there was no petrol available for miles and miles behind them, so turning back was simply not feasible. Despite what the police-man said (with sign-language and arm-waving) it had to be a better bet to press on *if* they could get through. The officer, perhaps with some experience of the mad British (and Irish), shrugged. They could try if they wanted to. Goods vehicles certainly couldn't get through but they might *just* be able to – if the petrol held out. Not many motorists have experienced this aspect of that particular situation. Messrs Carr, Smyth and Humphreys, their hearts beating in double time, now started to inch their way down the southern slope of the western Pyrenees – stomachs churning as the wheels scrabbled for a grip on the rubble which littered the single-track road with a sheer drop of hundreds of feet literally inches away from the car's off-side. Where the headlights showed a stretch of relatively clear road they switched off the engine and coasted, with all the dangers that *that* involves. If power had been required to take them round a bend or to avoid a fallen rock at any moment when they were cruising in neutral we might never have seen Warren, Roddy or Des again. Merciful Providence was on duty again that night. They got down the mountain and into a village just as the engine gave its final cough and died.

Don: All right. While running out of petrol is just about the daftest thing any motorist can do, we have to concede that the three in the Datsun also had their share of bad luck on that trip. But many of you must have contributed to your own misfortunes at times?

Ian: That's certainly true in my own case. It might be said, to some extent, of Jeff Hall when he and Ian Woosnam decided, eight or nine years ago, to do the tour in a converted single-decker bus. The passenger seats were removed and it was fitted out very comfortably with cooking and sleeping facilities, and altogether seemed to be a very good idea. The bus was thirty-six feet long and weighed eight and a half tons. What was not appreciated by the innovative Jeff was that to drive a vehicle of more than seven tons you need a special licence – or at least you do in Germany. Leaving Switzerland *en route* to the German Open, Jeff was stopped at the border and asked for the bus's documentation. It was then taken to a weighbridge, and suddenly the Polizei were talking in terms of a big fine for driving without the correct licence and for some mechanical fault they found with the bus. It was not often that the dire poverty of the sub-culture proved useful but this was the exception. When Jeff explained that he had no money to pay any fine he was simply shunted back into Switzerland, where he took another route to the *French* frontier. Here the guards were a little less thorough than their Teutonic colleagues and they confined their interest to the fact that he was driving with the wrong licence. Out of the blue appeared one of the circuit's caddies who, by the usual miracle which occurs on these occasions, just happened to have a heavy goods vehicle licence! He was allowed to drive the bus across the border and, better still, the party now got through to Germany, where Jeff played in the Open.

If that illustrates to some extent what a little persistence can do, consider now the case of Brian Sharrock, who has provided us with *the* classic story of life amongst the sub-culture. After years of trying, he finally got a bit of backing for a venture on to the circuit, starting in Madrid where, sadly but not surprisingly, he did not manage to pre-qualify. The next tournament was the Italian Open but, to make things a little trickier, that year the Italians had scheduled it to be played at Is Molas, which just happens to be at the southern end of the island of Sardinia. Not many of us had anything more than the most basic knowledge of the geography of Europe and I am sure Brian was no exception. He found his way to a seaport – Marseilles, I think it was – and took passage, after garaging the car, to the Mediterranean island. Unfortunately, the ship was heading for another one – Corsica.

Ah well. That, too, was an island in the Med. It shouldn't be too difficult to reach Sardinia. Brian, a determined Lancashire lad, hired a car and drove to the south of Corsica, from where he could actually *see* Sardinia; actually getting there was another matter because he now had to transfer from a French island to Italian soil. No problem. He went into a bar and, with much shouting and waving of arms (and the handing over of a franc or two) persuaded a local fisherman to sail him across the Straits of Bonifacio to Sardinia. So far, so good. But the fisherman was disinclined to get involved in such formalities as customs inspection and immigration checks, so he took the most practical course. He dropped Brian on a deserted beach in northern Sardinia. There he stood, with golf clubs and holdall, on a Sunday morning, with Is Molas still around 300 km away and a pre-qualifying round to be played there the following morning. Was he downhearted? Certainly not. He trudged up from the beach on to the nearest road and there he flagged down the first car to approach, the driver an Italian who spoke no English. After a prolonged multilingual discussion, the driver finally shrugged his shoulders in what Brian took to be a gesture of assent, so he piled his luggage on board and climbed into the passenger seat. The car drove 200 yards along the road, turned into the drive of a house and stopped. The driver had reached his home.

This series of adventures would have put off most people but not young Sharrock. He trudged back to the road and waited two hours for a bus to come along. It took him to a town where there was a railway station. A train transported him to the south of Sardinia and, after starting the day bargaining with a Corsican fisherman at 8 a.m., Brian finally reached Is Molas at eleven o'clock on the Sunday night – not in entirely the best shape and still with a pre-qualifying round to play, but his spirit was undaunted. And now his luck, it seemed, had changed.

Monday brought a continuous downpour and made the course unplayable. The organisers, with a field of eighty-seven pre-qualifiers for eighty places, decided to do the decent thing and scrub the pre-qualifying round altogether. At last he had made it. He was actually *in* his first European tournament. He could now compete with the best of them and, if his luck held, take home his first cheque. It would be nice to report that that happened. Alas, we cannot do so.

Brian was disqualified for an incorrect drop at a water hazard!

5 ![golfer icon] *More Horror Stories*

Don: Travel horror stories are not the exclusive preserve of the pre-qualifiers; they have involved some of the bigger names on the tournament circuit and our consultant in this field has got to be Randy Fox, an American who tried his hand at competitions in the 1970s and then decided that there was a more assured financial future in going into the travel business. He had seen enough disasters overtake his colleagues to know that there had to be a good market in selling packages to golfers who for many years had proved themselves constitutionally incapable of organising themselves around Europe. Clearly he has established himself as an expert in his new field but more than that, he is a gifted raconteur with an excellent memory. The stories just come tumbling out, endlessly. His first two suggest that some Australians are perhaps more resourceful than others.

Mike Ferguson – big, rough, tough Australian Mike, – had to travel from the Far Eastern circuit to Paris to pre-qualify for the French Open and had arranged to meet his wife in Singapore, but her flight was delayed and the meeting did not take place. Mike then had to face the fact that he had missed his connection to Paris and the only way he could now get there was on an Air France flight – via Moscow, with an overnight stop there! When he arrived in Moscow he had, of course, no visa and the Russians at that time did not take kindly to unexpected arrivals. No *glasnost*. They locked Mike away in a little four-by-two room with no ventilation and no heating. He was escorted to the plane for the onward flight the following morning, cold, cramped and hungry. He arrived at Paris about ten past nine for a nine-fifteen start and was not surprised when he failed to pre-qualify.

On another occasion the bus taking a party of players up

into the Alps for the Swiss Open at Crans-sur-Sierre broke
down on a steep slope and refused to restart. There was no
way of getting alternative transport and it was Rodger
Davis who found a solution to the problem. The luggage
was unloaded and spread across the road to form a barrier
so that any motorists driving to the resort had to stop. Each
one was politely required to take one golfer, and his
luggage, on to Crans-sur-Sierre in return for the barrier
being temporarily dismantled. It worked, too; everyone got
there on time.

The first trip I ever organised – I am surprised I survived
– was in 1979, to Vilamoura, and it was an unmitigated
disaster from start to finish. First of all the airlines were on
strike, including TAP (Portuguese Airways). They
borrowed a plane from British Airways and Tony Jacklin,
Howard Clark and the rest of those guys got there and were
due to stay in a block of flats. The staff got all the keys
mixed up so no one could get into the rooms which had
been allocated. Then there was another strike by members
of another union, which meant that nobody could have a
shave, and I remember Jacklin emerging from his room
with three days of designer stubble on his face – and he
wasn't happy about it. Then he was given incorrect
directions to a famous restaurant run by a British couple
and came back three hours and 120 miles later
complaining, 'I still can't find it.'

We chartered a plane to go on to the next tournament in
Malaga. On the way there, some of our South African
friends – Simon Hobday, Vinnie Baker and Bobby Lincoln
– started having a good time and making a bit of noise and
the pilot put a stop to that by announcing that if the party
didn't stop he would dump us back in Portugal. We
eventually got to Malaga, where Vinnie Baker got himself
arrested and I had to bail him out three days later. But I
had close to a hundred players staying in a rather good
hotel there and, of course, there was a strike of
hotel-workers on the Costa del Sol and all we had to eat for
three days was shredded lettuce. People were getting
thrown out of hotels and restaurants for being bombed

because of the drinking that was being done on empty stomachs.

Next, our party was declared overweight on a further leg of this tour from Italy to Lyons and we tried to get round this by averaging out the weight of a group of golfers with the weight of a party of forty nuns! Still the airport officials were not satisfied and they held back one ticket, insisting that one of our group would not fly unless he paid about £150 for excess baggage. It was Bernhard Langer's ticket which was withheld, and in those days he was a pre-qualifier, not making much money. But somehow, in the end, he got to France.

I've always had a soft spot for Sweden – they treat us like kings up there, the discos are fine and there's sun all day long. Everybody's healthy and happy in the summer time. We were up there in a little town called Lidkoping which was just unbelievable. There was a young player who worked for me – I won't mention his name – and he had never been to Sweden before. I warned him to be careful, but sure enough, on the first night he met a six-foot-tall lady race-car driver and went home with her. Next morning he was due to tee-off at eight-ten, and at eight-twenty-five he came crawling through the bushes in the same clothes he was wearing the night before and was disqualified for missing his tee-time. What the hell – he spent the rest of the week with her! The famous stories of the girls coming up and grabbing you and taking you away – it doesn't often happen any more, but that's what happened in Lidkoping on that occasion. You've got to be quick off the mark, though. There was one of our friends from the southern part of Africa who met this beautiful blonde and told her he'd like to spend the night with her. She said, 'I will, but I don't like beards, so if you go and shave yours off, we'll take it from there.' He rushed up to his room, ripped his face to shreds in his haste and came tumbling down the stairs with a baby-white complexion, spattered with blood. She'd gone off with someone else.

I guess no talk with me would be complete without recalling one of those occasions when I have gone completely mad, screaming and shouting and throwing things about. It takes a visit to Italy to do that. There was a complete revolt of the players when we arrived for the Italian Open at a beautiful little island south of Venice and found that our apartments were brand new and had never been used. In fact the heat had never been turned on, the doors had never been closed, there was two inches of water in most of the rooms and if you ran your hand over the beds it came up wet. I found the agent drinking champagne in the clubhouse, good old Mario, and when I complained he lost his cool and shouted *at me*: 'I'm not a goddam travel agent.' He said it just as my glass of wine arrived and I threw it at him. I guess I shouldn't have done that because glasses are expensive.

I think Italy is best summed up by an experience I had when George O'Grady (of the PGA) and I were sitting having lunch at Monza on a Tuesday and we went up to get our dessert from the buffet. Immediately, ninety-six waiters came running out saying, 'You mustn't get dessert. *We* will serve it to you.' OK, fine. We sat down and they served the course. The next day, Wednesday, George and I were having lunch again and we called over the waiter and asked him to get our sweet. He made a big deal about this and said they weren't allowed to get us our sweet. So George protested, 'Yesterday you said we weren't allowed to get sweet. Today you say we must get it ourselves. What's going on?' And then the waiter gave us the words which for me sum up exactly the Italian way of handling everything: 'Yesterday was yesterday. Today is today.'

At Waterloo, in Belgium, Peter Barber won a BMW for a hole in one, the biggest prize he had ever won; it was bright orange, about £20,000 worth. Just as the prize ceremony was about to begin an incredible rainstorm started and we all fled into the clubhouse. When the rain stopped about an hour later and everybody emerged, the car had been stolen! They did replace it, I'm glad to say. But for even more barefaced daylight robbery, take the case of Rodger Davis, playing in Switzerland. He marked his ball with a five-franc piece and went up to take a look at the spike marks round

the hole. When he returned, the coin had been
nicked.

Organising travel and accommodation throws up
problems you never dreamed about – guys snoring, for
instance. I've had players come to me with their eyes falling
out of their head and complaining, 'Look, I had to sleep in
the bathtub last night with a pillow tied round my head.
You've got to get me away from that chap I'm rooming
with.' Then you get the accident-prone players. There was
the young fellow who dropped his contact-lens into a bowl
of spaghetti and then ate it. A week later he got
food-poisoning and when they were taking him to hospital
someone stole all his luggage. He quit the tour and went
over to the States skiing. He broke his leg.

In Cape Town I had a guy come to me and complain,
'I'm completely exhausted.' 'How's that?' I asked. 'Well,'
he said, 'my room-mate's had a girl there for four days and
it's impossible for me to get any sleep.'

You would be amazed at the number of players who leave
a tournament thinking they have missed the halfway cut
when in fact they haven't. One actually had to fly back to
France to play his third round after coming home. Another
player we got flagged down by police on the M4 and
directed back to the course. The one man who would never
do that is Brian Marchbank. If you ask Brian in the middle
of the second day what the cut-figure is going to be he will
tell you *exactly*. Don't ask me how he does it, but he's never
wrong.

Some funny things happen in Madrid. We were staying
at the Palace Hotel, a favourite of ours, and we were setting
off in a bus for the course one morning. Around the main
plaza between the hotel and the Prado the main cargo door
flew open and the cry went up from the back of the bus,
'Hey, a set of clubs just fell out in the main traffic lane.'
Tony Jacklin growled, 'They've got to be mine.' Sure
enough, they were – all over the street, but not one was run
over and you know what the traffic is like in the centre of
Madrid! Another year, it was about 75 or 80 degrees on the
day we arrived and young Jeremy Bennett decided he

would play in shorts. Now, Jeremy is never ahead of time –
he always arrives just as the bus doors are about to close –
and on the second day he came dashing out in his short blue
shorts and white knee stockings, looking very sharp indeed.
But the temperature had dropped to 31 degrees – from heat
to absolute, raw cold. His knees started to turn red as he
walked across the pavement, but he dared not miss the bus.
He finished the day playing in his waterproofs.

I don't normally handle travel arrangements for caddies.
They live in a world all of their own. They have their own
methods, their own language, their own way of life. And
they know each other, not by the names which appear on
passports or electoral rolls, but by the strangest collection of
nicknames you will ever meet – no Tom, Dick or Harry in
the caddies' world. So I was a bit surprised when Manuel
Pinero's caddy came to me one day and asked if I would
book a party of ten of them on a trip to Sweden. I pointed
out that the Swedish trip was expensive, but that if they
wanted to put the money up-front I would make the
bookings. Now, how would you like to give this list of names
to British Airways? The Stuntman, the Brain, the Professor,
Fish Fingers, Edinburgh Jimmy, Crazy Gus, Wobbly – oh
boy! But they're good guys, and there are some very
colourful stories about the way they travel.

6 The Caddies

Don: Largely because of television, I suppose, some of the top caddies have become quite well-known to the golfing public. Peter Alliss, in particular, often identifies them in his commentary and I must say that when I was working on radio commentary there were many occasions when I had reason to be grateful to them. It adds something to the description of play if one can mention the club a player has used, and over the years I developed a simple system with most of the top caddies of getting a hand-signal which identified the club (it could perhaps be a little ambiguous when the two-iron was in use). Only once have I ever questioned a caddy's word, and that was during a World Match-Play tournament at Wentworth, when Ballesteros's brother Vicente was carrying the bag. On that immensely long seventeenth hole (something like 560 or 570 yards), Sevvy's tee-shot hit the trees on the left and rebounded into the light rough. I hurried on ahead and took up position in front of one of the splendid gardens which flank the fairway and noted with some envy that a pre-lunch champagne party was taking place on the terrace of a desirable mod. res. Sevvy's second shot duly arrived, stopping yards from the putting surface, and the thought flitted through my mind, 'One iron? three wood?'

Sevvy and Vicente marched forward towards the green and, catching the caddy's eye, I held up one finger with my features contorted into what I hoped was a suitably interrogative expression. Vicente smiled delightedly and shook his head; beyond that he was clearly not yet disposed to offer further clues. As Sevvy had advanced to inspect the green there was time for further charades. I held up two fingers. No. Three? No. It couldn't be a four, surely? My hesitation at last found a sympathetic response. With a huge grin of pure joy, Vicente showed me all the fingers and thumb of one hand and three

fingers of the other. Eight? That was impossible. He *couldn't*
have covered around 550 yards with a drive and an eight iron.
Incredulously, I thought out loud, 'An eight. It *can't* be,' and at
that moment one of the stewards accompanying the match
passed by and overheard: 'It was an eight-iron,' he said. 'I saw
it.' Three minutes later, as I informed Radio 2 listeners of
the reduction of the Burma Road's seventeenth by Severiano
Ballesteros to a drive and an eight-iron I wondered how many
of them muttered, 'Silly sod. He's got it wrong.' Sevvy's
brothers are all useful golfers, one of them (Manuel) a pretty
successful tournament player and they have all done some
caddying for the star of the family at one time or another.

Do expert golfers make good caddies or are they, perhaps, too
subjective to do as professional a job as the full-time *professional*
caddy with a more objective approach? It's a point I have often
pondered, especially when you see the top players of the circuit
in consultation with the top caddies.

Ian: Perhaps I can give you an idea of how useful – no,
invaluable – the best of them can be. As we went into the last
tournament of the 1983 season, the Portuguese, I was lying
sixtieth in the Order of Merit. If I stayed there I would be
'exempt' for the circuit in 1984; if I drifted out to sixty-first or
worse I would be back on the treadmill of trying simply to get
into the following year's tournaments by playing a pre-
qualifying round. I didn't want to go back to those days at any
price. Everyone from fifty-fifth to seventieth would be trying
like mad in Portugal, and all would be highly motivated, so I
had to be sure. At the end of the preceding tournament in
Barcelona I heard that Sevvy would not be playing in Portugal
and therefore his caddy, Peter Coleman, had no engagement.
Pete is the top man. At that time, before Langer climbed to the
top, Pete had only worked for Sevvy and for Greg Norman. He
was the best. So with great diffidence, I approached him.

Don: Wait a minute – let's get this into perspective. You
are saying that you, a tournament player of eleven years'
experience, were in something like awe of a caddy?

Ian: Absolutely. In *my* job, I was a struggling sixtieth; Pete
Coleman, in his job, was number one. I was indeed in awe, and
I didn't know how he would react. In the event, I found him a

pleasant and approachable guy and he listened while I explained my position, then agreed to do it. Next we came to the matter of wages and he asked for the same as Sevvy paid him: £120 a week and 5 per cent of any prize money. I replied, 'That's very fair, but 5 per cent of me is not going to be quite the same as 5 per cent of Sevvy. I'll pay you £120 for the week and 20 per cent of prize money.' Pete said, 'You don't have to but it's a very fair offer. Thank you.' So off we went in our various ways to Troia, forty miles south of Lisbon and one of the most difficult courses on the circuit. Pete was there on the dot, on the Tuesday before the Open began on the Thursday, and we went out for a practice round.

I had an old, beaten-up golf bag which served to make me feel even more the junior partner in the team. I felt I was lucky to get him and I was now prepared to place myself entirely in his hands. We hit lots of balls from different places; he had a good look at my game and at the course, calculating his own yardages. At the last hole, a big par-five, I spun a ball off the front and tried a couple of further wedge shots, neither of which quite got the ball up to the hole, although the yardage seemed to suggest that a wedge was the right club. Pete said nothing until we left the course, then he asked, 'How far do you hit a wedge?' and my answer was 'Between 110 and 120 yards.' He observed, 'It doesn't seem to be going that far. Let's go and try out your clubs.' At that time I was playing a mild steel chrome-plated iron. Most guys play them. They are made of quite soft steel and with the amount of golf we play, the amount of loft and lie varies during a season; we have to have them checked and adjusted a couple of times a season. Sure enough, when we checked we found that my wedge was too lofted and consequently I could only hit it about ninety-five yards. I had not questioned this and had just assumed it was carrying the ball the distance I expected. Pete went with me to the practice ground with a pedometer, and after I had hit several balls with every club in the bag he checked the distances. That was just the beginning of his professionalism: to carry out his duties to his own standards he first of all had to know how far I hit the ball with each club. That was something I had never done myself; I just *assumed*.

I shot 74, 74 on what is perhaps the hardest course I have ever played, and I was lying eighth after two rounds. So far, so good. I had made the cut. But so had everyone else who was competing with me for a place in the top sixty of the Order of Merit: Peter Teravainen, John O'Leary, John Morgan, Roger Chapman, Nick Job. In the third round I was paired with O'Leary and Sam Torrance; he was the defending champion and so we took with us the only crowd of the day – Troica is a bit off the beaten track and the event was not well supported. One of the hardest features of the course is that there is no semi-rough. There are a few trees but lots of very soft sand beside the tight fairways, so that when you take a gallery with you the sand quickly gets churned up and has deep footmarks. This was the moment I chose to lose my game and continually hit the ball wide. Every time it went into these sandy verges it seemed to finish in the deepest of the footmarks. I had to blast recovery shots simply to get back on the fairway.

Sometimes I was so wide that I had to play out on to another fairway, and that made it difficult in the extreme for my caddy to work out a yardage (they are calculated from the middle of our own fairways, of course). Any resemblance to the sort of prize-money percentage he got from Sevvy and what he was going to get from me was now far out of sight and if Pete had simply shrugged his shoulders and let me flounder into further disaster I certainly couldn't have blamed him. It was only some time after the tournament that I realised the full extent of his professionalism. If he had been caddying for Ballesteros he could have been no more painstaking or protective. He kept the bag on his shoulder and never even let me near a club until he had settled me down and done absolutely everything by the book. He would turn up with the bag, *and* the yardage *and* enough simple, positive information to enable me to work out the shot. He's a pleasant, placid sort of chap with a good calming influence. I shot 79, 80 in those last two rounds and tied for thirty-second place; if I had taken one shot more I would have been in trouble. How, then, can I say that Pete Coleman's influence was all-important? Just this: I made that sixtieth place in the 1983 Order of Merit *because* he was there and because of the way he handled me. Without him I wouldn't have done it.

There is one further point worth dwelling on from Troia, 1983. It was the only time I had been in that stressful situation. I had missed the top sixty in the first seven years on the circuit and never even been in contention. Then, in 1980, 1981 and 1982 I had been comfortably inside the top sixty and I certainly didn't want to lose my exemption. Consequently, this was the first time I had felt pressure of this kind. I shared a room with Maurice Bembridge and so there was a marked absence of the cumulative paranoia which might have resulted if I had been sharing with someone in the same bracket as myself. Maurice is a lovely, relaxed, pipe-smoking character who wore pyjamas (unheard of in my circles!) and read P. G. Wodehouse in bed. This was after his nightly visit to the mudflats near the course. Maurice is a keen ornithologist and each evening he would take his notebooks and his binoculars out to the estuary and sit contentedly studying the birdlife – a wonderful calming influence and I was grateful for it.

Don: Well, we've heard one aspect of the caddying profession and Randy Fox gave us a glimpse of these boys from a completely different angle. Some of them must have had travelling adventures as way out as those experienced by the sub-culture?

Ian: None better than John O'Reilly when he was caddying for Peter Townsend. The German Open has only once been staged in Berlin, so there was no precedent for travel arrangements to that venue. It might have helped a few people if they had had a slight knowledge of geography, or politics or even post-war history. Anyway, after finishing the Irish Open in Portmarnock, Peter arranged to meet his caddy the following week in Berlin and John O'Reilly set out with a band of his fellows for Germany. On the crossing from Dublin to Liverpool the caddies had a card school and Mr O'Reilly lost all his wages. The party contrived a lift to Hull for the voyage to the Hook of Holland, and John still had the best part of 1,000 miles to go with no money. Somehow he got on board ship and by a similar sort of miracle he disembarked in Holland. Now he only had the train-journey to Berlin – or so the party thought. That was no problem. John was wrapped in the coverall, property of P. Townsend, and parked on the luggage-rack of their compartment while his mates settled down for the journey to Berlin.

What had escaped everyone's notice was that the former German capital is deep in the heart of *East* Germany, and so it came as something of a shock when the train stopped and frontier-guards invaded the train. However, that passed off qutie well; passports were stamped and the luggage was not inspected, but just as the train was about to move off someone in the party had the presence of mind to work out that if John O'Reilly tried to exit *from* East Germany in due course (they hadn't worked out the details of the return journey at that stage; the important thing was to get to the German Open and do their duty) there would be no entry visa on his passport and the frontier guards had not seemed overburdened with a sense of humour. They might not understand. John leapt down (with assistance) from the luggage-rack, borrowed a train ticket from one of his pals, chased after the guards and had his passport franked. He was in. Fortunately for John, he had a HGV licence and so, for the return trip, he volunteered to drive the PGA mobile office and all was well – until he took a wrong turning and found himself in the off-limits area of East Berlin! Now he was involved with the Russians as well as the East Germans – John was locked up for the night. But after a lot of telephoning (the office was required at the following tournament, the Swiss Open) driver and vehicle were released from custody and J. O'Reilly, having arrived in East Germany concealed in a golf-bag coverall, drove out in style with a motor-cycle escort.

Great improvisers the Irish. Christy O'Connor (Himself) had for many years a quaint character of a caddy called Tiny who decided to save on accommodation costs during a tournament at Lindrick (Notts) by kipping down in an old shed he had spotted not far from the clubhouse. Unfortunately he fell asleep while smoking a cigarette and Sod's Law decreed that instead of smouldering harmlessly away, the cigarette set fire to, and burned down, the whole issue. Next morning, as players and public surveyed the smoking ruins with mild interest Tiny reported for duty in clobber which bore unmistakable signs of having been fairly recently in close proximity to a conflagration of some kind. But he knew nothing about the fire. No surs, nothing at all.

Jimmy Scouse and Podgy were two famous old characters of the caddy circuit who were also keen to live as economically as possible, at least when it came to a place to rest their heads. At Fulford, after a certain amount of celebration, they decided to sleep it off in one of the large skips used to cart away rubbish at the end of the day's play, and so soundly did the two sleep that they missed the arrival of the transporter truck. I am happy to report that they woke up before being actually dumped on the Corporation refuse tip.

Don: When, in 1959, the *Daily Mail* invited me to stop playing cricket and to start writing about it, a problem arose. I had retired from rugby football two years previously and a ball game seemed as necessary to me as breathing. Golf seemed a reasonable alternative and with naive arrogance I assumed that hitting a stationary Dunlop 65 presented no more difficulties than hitting a moving spheroid of larger dimensions. Disillusionment on this score was delayed for a year or two, however, because the hospitable Bradford League club, Undercliffe, offered me the opportunity of continuing to play cricket on Sundays. They had a highly competitive selection of friendly fixtures, played on a day which was available to me, and there was no nonsense about any of them. We don't play it for fun in Yorkshire, and I was not yet ready for any more genteel form of cricket than the cut-throat stuff I had been born and bred to play. But after years of commuting to and fro between the family home in Manchester and the playing fields of West Yorkshire it gradually became more of a wrench to leave behind my wife and our two growing sons on the one day of the week when I could reasonably expect to be with them on a fairly regular basis. A new alternative presented itself in the form of the TV All-Stars team, founded and organised by Michael Parkinson and Bill Grundy, who both at that time worked for Granada Television, based in Manchester. Parkie was a good and enthusiastic player, reared in Barnsley's Yorkshire League side; Bill was adept at roping in various celebrities to accompany the side to venues (mostly around the north-west) and to join in these fund-raising occasions. The Coronation Street crowd were particularly good at coming along to sign autographs and to mingle with the crowds, and we were joined from time to time by other Granada personnel who have since gone on to more distinguished careers in television and showbiz.

One of our most regular supporters from 'The Street' was the flame-haired Sandra Gough, at that time performing as Irma Ogden, daughter of Stan and Hilda. She was a delightful Sunday afternoon companion and a great trouper, willingly (if not always happily) dispensing kisses at five bob a time during the tea interval to augment the gate receipts substantially. This led to her describing Bill Grundy (who first announced the kisses-for-sale venture without Sandra's knowledge or consent) as 'a sexy pig', an expression which pleased her so much that she dispensed it almost as regularly as her chaste salutations. She once applied it to the Rt. Hon. Harold Wilson, MP when she encountered him on an electioneering safari in Liverpool, delighting the Prime Minister of Great Britain and Northern Ireland, startling his immediate companion, Peregrine Worsthorne, and providing Parkie with one of his favourite stories.

Our cricketing companions and aficionados included Jimmy Saville, Johnny Hamp, the gifted producer of popular music programmes who played a major role in the developing careers of the Beatles, and the occasional 'borrowed' professional cricketer from the Leagues, such as Eddie Barlow and Bob Bartels. One of our regulars was a chap called Eddie Luckarift, who religiously turned up every Sunday in a black Humber Hawk saloon, which became generally known as the Hearse. Eddie, a grey-haired and middle-aged bachelor cricket 'nut', arrived for each game wearing a startling blazer in which purple seemed the predominant colour, but with generous supporting hues of yellow and black. He also wore a white silk cravat, giving him the general appearance of an off-duty Battle of Britain pilot who had remustered as a rock salesman on Cleethorpes promenade. No one ever really seemed to know what Eddie did for a living. Grundy introduced him, week by week, in differing roles which varied between script-writer of 'The Epilogue' to next week's star guest on 'The Simon Dee Show'. No matter how many games I played with him in the All Stars team, and for years afterwards when I encountered him from time to time in the BBC's Northern headquarters, I never discovered what he did to earn a crust, although he once confided that he and a partner had staged a summer show on Morecambe's Central Pier and had lost money on it. This came as no great surprise since a show written collectively by Rodgers and Hammerstein, Lerner and Loewe, Rice and Lloyd-Webber with additional music and lyrics from Sondheim would undoubtedly be a flop in Morecambe. Mr Luckarift, however, did achieve a place in the folklore of the All Stars.

We had strayed across the Pennines for a game in Chesterfield during which a pretty young thing, hoping, no doubt, to make the acquaintance of one or more of the burgeoning disc jockeys who swelled our ranks, spent most of the afternoon in or around the All Stars' dressing-room. As the immediate object of her interest had brought along his current girlfriend there was going to be no joy for her in that quarter but she was a trier, one had to say that. At close of play we enjoyed the customary local hospitality for an hour or so and then set out for a pre-arranged rendezvous on the way back to our respective homes in the Manchester area. When we all assembled in a pub in Disley, fairly close to Stockport and thus an awfully long way from Chesterfield, we discovered that Eddie (also a trier) had the pretty young thing in tow and was clearly hoping to have his wicked way with her at some later stage. Round about midnight (it was that sort of excellent pub) it finally became clear to Eddie that there was to be no joy for him and that simple courtesy – we were, if nothing else a gentlemanly bunch in the early sixties – as well as an age-gap of rather obvious proportions demanded that Eddie get the Hearse on the road back to Chesterfield.

With a chorus of mock sympathy ringing in his ears he nobly ventured forth, only to drive off the road on the Derbyshire hills so that he and the pretty young thing woke up the following morning in a Buxton hospital. Fortunately no serious damage was done, but it was thought necessary to keep the young lady in for an extra day for observation while Eddie was discharged. First, however, he was instructed to present himself to the Matron. There, with a fine mixture of disapproval and disgust, the formidable lady addressed herself to Eddie: 'You can go home. But I have a message from your, er, girlfriend. *She wants you to ring her headmistress to explain why she will not be in for school today.*'

The Hearse was repaired and the pair of them resumed their

travels with the All Stars, but it was a chastened and subdued
Eddie after that, although he did bring off one blinding catch in
a game at Birkenhead Park which brought the house down.
Parkie went off to fame and fortune in London and the All Stars
broke up. We had raised a lot of money for various children's
charities and although the cricket never reached high levels of
competitiveness, at least we had our memories.

It was time for me to find an alternative ball game and my
thoughts turned again to golf. My wife had played since she was
eleven years old – getting progressively worse, it seemed, but
enjoying the fresh air and exercise – and Ian was now making
rather good progress as a twelve-year-old. If they could play the
game I was quite sure I could. Also, it would enable me to join
in the Sunday (day off) activities of the Yorkshire cricket team,
with whom I was usually deployed by the *Daily Mail* since they
were a regular championship-winning team and we sold a lot of
papers in the broad acres by having regular match reports, plus
a weekly cricket gossip column. With no Sunday League until
1969, the Sabbath was always very definitely golf day, and all
round the country there were hospitable clubs who offered the
courtesy of the course to county cricketers (and assorted camp-
followers) playing in their vicinity. This was astonishingly
generous when one thinks of how much Sunday means to the
average club golfer and we must have shocked and horrified an
entire generation of players who smilingly stood back and
waved us on to the first tee ahead of the waiting multitude.

There *were* competent golfers amongst our number, notably
Brian Close, Ken Taylor and Jim Kilburn, cricket correspondent of the *Yorkshire Post*, but the remainder, for the most part,
were a motley collection of hedgers-and-ditchers in the more
extreme regions of incompetence. Divots were dug from first
tees all over the country; scuffed shots trickled into rho-
dodendron clumps or whistled at tangents through windows of
imposing clubhouses. Experienced and expert golfers far and
wide gazed to the heavens and whistled softly through clenched
teeth as they contemplated hours of waiting behind bizarre
groups of four who were already hard at it, desecrating and
destroying their fairways. Worcester was a favourite port of
call; the Golf and Country Club nobly tolerated us for many

years. So did the Finchley Golf Club when we were in London.
(Once, grossly ill-advisedly, Closey organised a mass visit to
Wentworth and years later, commentating there, I have mar-
velled at the way the course has recovered from that visit. We
were never invited to return.) On Yorkshire's very occasional
visits to Dover, Jim Swanton hospitably arranged golf for the
more competent members of the party at some of the great
courses in the Sandwich area, largely, I suspect, because of his
friendship with Jim Kilburn. Those who were invited to these
occasions returned refreshed by the sea breezes and stimulated
by the quality of the courses, but just a teeny bit miffed by the
time it took to complete a round which was invariably punctu-
ated by introduction to at least three peers of the realm and a
selection of rear-admirals, air marshals and a lieutenant-
general or two!

Brian Close, a brilliant golfer both right-handed (initially)
and then left-handed, was a tigerish opponent in any company.
When he first took up the game he was warned, mischievously
by Len Hutton and Denis Compton, that it might have an
adverse effect upon his left-handed batting so Close, scarcely
out of his teens, began as a right-handed golfer. In a very short
time indeed he was playing off two! Then, playing in the Gibson
Cup (a competition for Yorkshire players and committee, past
and present) he found himself with a bit of a wait on the tee at a
par-three hole and borrowed one of Johnny Wardle's left-
handed irons. After hitting one or two shots sweetly from the
alien stance he completed his round, went into the pro's shop
and ordered a set of left-handed clubs. Inside a year he was
playing off five! I thought I knew just about everything there
was to know about my friend Brian Close but in the mid-
seventies, while 'ghosting' his autobiography, I found in his
mother's scrapbook an account by Ben Wright (once the *Daily
Mirror*'s golf correspondent, now for many years a noted TV
commentator in the USA) of a round they played together at
Moortown, Leeds. Close played the odd-numbered holes left-
handed with his own clubs and the even numbers right-handed,
using Ben's. Try to imagine, if you will, the difficulties a round
like that presents, especially on a championship course (the
Brabazon Trophy, the Car-Care Plan tournament have been

played there) and golfers will immediately see Close's score of 76 – five over par – as an astonishing achievement.

But what a competitor! He once went out with Ken Taylor for an early-morning round on one of the Bristol courses with one set of clubs (Closey's) between them. Taylor was to receive six shots. After four holes Close found himself two down with only one of Taylor's shots gone; he immediately 'docked' the remaining shots that Ken was due to receive. At the turn Brian was three down and at that point (as a head-shaking Taylor reported over breakfast) he decreed, 'Bugger this. You can't use my woods from now on.' That's the spirit which honed York-shire's keen edge of competitiveness. Close brought to golf the same belief in his own indestructibility which was a hallmark of his close-to-the-wicket fielding in cricket or his batting against Wes Hall and Charlie Griffith at Lord's in 1963. Playing in a pro–celebrity–am–am at the Cambridgeshire Club in a team of left-handers (the pro was Bob Charles), Brian struck prime form over the opening holes. Then, after dragging a tee shot slightly into light rough, he forged on ahead of his three partners, forgetting that some people do not hit the ball quite as far as he does. Consequently, he should not have been entirely surprised to find himself struck on the back of the head when one of his amateur partners played a three-wood from the fair-way about twenty-five yards behind him. (The etiquette of all this might have been less than perfect but that's another matter altogether). 'Good God,' I exclaimed, as Closey told me the story. 'Were you all right?' 'No, I wasn't,' snarled the iron man of cricket. 'I dropped three bloody shots on the next four holes.'

Fred Trueman tells the story of a group of ex-cricketers discussing prowess on the golf course and reaching the unani-mous conclusion that the best in modern times – perhaps of all time – has been Ted Dexter. Close, who up to that point had taken no part in the debate, suddenly intervened. 'You what?' he demanded. 'Dexter? I've played him right-handed and I've played him left-handed and I've beaten him both times.'

Like most of his fellow-countrymen, Brian firmly believed that if it was quite impossible to get something for nothing he would reluctantly settle for paying out as little as possible. This applied particularly to green fees. At one time in the seventies

he worked for the Bell Fruit gaming machine company and part
of his duties was to persuade brewery directors, or individual
licensees, to place machines in their pubs. Brian found it
particularly pleasant to carry out these negotiations during a
round of golf – who wouldn't? – so it became his custom to fix an
appointment at a convenient course, then seek out a friend who
was a member there and invite him to get himself a partner to
play Closey and his client – at a reduced green fee because he
was playing with a member! He would then ring his bookmaker
before starting the round, put £100 on a horse without batting
an eyelid, and play golf with joy in his heart that it was costing
£5 instead of £20. For business appointments in Lancashire he
expected me to drop whatever I was doing, find a friend who
was a member at Formby, Southport and Ainsdale, or wher-
ever -- who then had to drop whatever *he* was doing – and sally
forth on to the course in the long-term interests of the Bell Fruit
Company. Thus it was that I played Formby, the magnificent
course just south of Southport, for the first time and somewhere
about the seventeenth I found myself in a position (which rarely
occurred) to win a hole. The other three all drove out of bounds
into a wood on the right of the fairway. Not knowing that
Formby incorporates a ladies' course as well, I struggled
heroically over a strangely long and strangely shaped hole to
'win' with a seven. At that point my friend marched back,
played three off the tee and got down in six, but in a different
area from the one where I had completed *my* hole. Then, and
only then, did he inform me that I had holed out on the sixth
green of the ladies' course and my brief hour of glory was at an
end. Oh yes – a great competitor, D. B. Close.

Lest it be thought that I regard myself as in any way a fit
golfing companion for any of the great names which appear in
these pages, let me say at this point that, being naturally idle, I
have never taken a lesson in the game and I have never spent
one second in a practice area. It all shows. At one stage I got
down to twelve handicap but this was due more to needless
fears in the minds of the Denton GC handicap committee than
any realistic view of my ability. At the same time, let it also be
noted that because I had played cricket for about thirty years
when I joined the Denton Club, where my wife and son played,

that same committee insisted that I start with an eighteen handicap; no club since then has been generous enough to give me a figure better than that. Consequently, my modest golfing life has been one long struggle.

Through the misguided generosity of many people, however, I have been invited to desecrate some of the great courses of the world, especially since the Celebrity am–am has become such a splendid fund-raising enterprise of cricket beneficiaries and a number of charities. My most ambitious venture was when I was invited to play in the inaugural pro–am on the eve of the Benson and Hedges International tournament at Fulford, York, and in a moment of over-ambitious enthusiasm accepted. There followed four nightmare weeks in which I contemplated making a complete fool of myself in front of thousands of people, and my fears were enhanced when I was drawn to play with José Maria Canizares plus two guests of the sponsors. I consulted my son. 'It's quite simple,' he replied, consolingly. 'When you've played your first six shots, pick up your ball and let the pro get on with his job.' That was, of course, a great help!

Came the day, and the rain poured mercilessly. The other two amateurs in our group had even higher handicaps than mine and we uneasily confessed to each other on the first tee that while we didn't fancy our chances of setting a course record when dressed in light shirts and slacks, the prospects of doing so were considerably diminished when accoutred in sweaters and waterproofs as well. In abject terror we contemplated a crowd of several hundred people funnelling away from the first tee, not one of them apparently realising that he was in mortal danger. Alternating between gibbering terror and arrant cowardice, I took a five-wood off the tee and almost fainted with relief as I hit what would have been a caught-and-bowled sitter in a game I knew a little more about. At least it had gone straight; no one was being carried away with blood streaming down his face. Things did not improve substantially over the next seventeen holes. As we gathered on each tee and the pro – a charming and scrupulously courteous man – took out the card and inquired, 'Score please?' we looked at him with fixed smiles and offered, 'Six – net five,' 'Seven – net six.' With a small sad and almost imperceptible shake of the head, Señor Canizares gravely recorded these modest achievements and re-started play. I actually hit the green at the short fourteenth (where a car is usually offered for a hole-in-one during the tournament-proper) but took another three to get down; one of my fellow-sufferers managed a net five at a long hole and that, as I remember it, was the full extent of our collective contribution.

Our team score of level par was a marvellous tribute to the steadiness and steadfastness of the pro; it contrasted poorly with the 24-under return of the winners, Sam Torrance and his merry men. Nor was there the entertainment that I expected from the four following us round the course in which the pro was Tommy Bolt, the American, and the celebrity my good friend F. S. Trueman – two of the world's more volatile golfers. For the first three or four holes I cast apprehensive glances behind us, expecting to see angrily hurled clubs flying in our direction, but the rain put a damper even on that.

Yet *some* good obviously came out of the experience, at least as far as the pro was concerned. Shortly afterwards Canizares won the Bob Hope Classic and went on to a fair number of European victories. Occasionally I met him around courses and clubhouses and on the first couple of occasions I accosted him with a bright smile and the comment, 'That lesson I gave you at Fulford has obviously been very useful indeed, hasn't it?' The look of non-comprehending bewilderment which greeted this crude, fumbling attempt at humour could only have been captured by one other man – that marvellous actor John Le Mesurier, master of the deadpan expression and Sergeant Wilson in 'Dad's Army'.

A few years ago I was invited to join the great Irish and Lions rugby captain, Willie John McBride, as a guest speaker at the New Zealand Sportsman of the Year dinner in Auckland. After flying us in luxuriously, the organising committee invited us to play a round of golf on the morning before the dinner. My partner, Leo, and I somehow contrived to win on the last green and as a few dollars changed hands over a beer or two, Willie John (a banker) inquired with engaging ingenuousness, 'Will I pay you in Irish punts?' 'What's that?' asked my partner and I hastily intervened to warn him, 'They are worth about four-pence-ha'penny apiece. Don't touch 'em.' Leo, however, was a businessman, too. 'If you'll autograph the punts, I'll take them,' he ventured. W.J. duly obliged and Leo was able to auction the notes for around a hundred dollars a time that evening, with the proceeds going to the Murray Halberg Trust, for which the dinner was being staged.

A round of golf often comes as a blessed relief in the middle of a long England cricket tour, even if it involves playing in somewhat alien conditions with borrowed clubs. The Officers' Club, Rawalpindi, gave us a good start to the 1977–8 tour, with Ken Barrington, the manager (and an excellent player), giving his game an airing along with Ian Botham, Mike Gatting and a few others. It would be reasonably easy to get one's handicap down in Pakistan since each player has not only a caddy but a couple of ballboys as well to patrol the fairways a flattering distance ahead, one on either flank. No ball ever has to be played out of the jungle. Having seen the tee-shot disappear over mid-wicket or extra cover, the player advances pessimistically down the course only to find the ball sitting up neatly on a convenient tussock, on the edge of the fairway but very definitely in play. The boys do their work well. It was after coming in from such a round that I found myself contemplating one of the saddest sights I have ever seen in a golf club – a bar behind which the shelves were completely empty save for one, solitary bottle of 'Seven-up' mineral water. Pakistan is, publicly, a 'dry' country. But the course had been in pretty good condition, with hordes of khaki-clad figures working busily all around, so when we were greeted (over tea and toast) by the dignitaries of the Officers' Club we were able to say with complete honesty, 'May we compliment you, Mr Captain, on the state of the course?' A lieutenant-colonel of the Pakistan army beamed with delight before replying, deprecatingly, 'Thank you, gentlemen. You are very kind. But, you know, when a club has forty-three members and 30,000 green-keeping staff it is not too difficult to keep things in good order.' Even in Pakistan, the army knows how to look after itself.

It was in Calcutta in 1982 that Graham Gooch holed in one, playing in a match behind me, and to the best of my knowledge no one has had a drink to this day to mark the occasion. It was in Delhi on the same tour that I first experienced really acute homesickness on a tour. Frank Keating, of the *Guardian*, had somehow managed to organise a supply of Buck's Fizz to greet Christmas morning, and as I looked out from his room onto the Royal Delhi GC I thought of the years of Ian's boyhood when the two of us always played a round at the start of the Christmas holiday. Never on any tour have I experienced a comparable sense of loss at being so far away from my family.

With my other son (primarily a rugby man and resident in Australia) I played an intriguing round on the Moore Park Club, close to Sydney Cricket Ground. We started out behind two schoolboys playing with one set of clubs. As they invariably drove to opposite sides of the course, progress was laboured and it was not helped when, halfway round, a *five*-ball suddenly appeared behind us from cars parked on a main road which runs through the course and started booming healthy tee-shots over our heads and around our ears. It was nerve-racking to say the least. Somehow we survived and as we returned the hired clubs to the pro he inquired, matily, 'Owditgowthin?' 'Interest-ing,' I replied in my frostiest Pom-to-Colonial accent. 'Interest-ing?' he queried, 'Owsthit?' 'Well,' I replied loftily, 'it is the first time I have tried to play golf on a course in a complete state of anarchy.' He was clearly not disposed to debate the point. 'Suityerself,' he commented tersely and applied himself to more pressing matters.

The West Indies provides a number of courses of widely differing qualities, ranging from Sandy Lane in the millionaire belt of Barbados (where a bus transports you from ninth green to tenth tee and whatever you pay the caddies is never enough) to the magnificent Caymanas Park, Jamaica, where we encoun-tered a squad of police carrying away a case of rifles which had been dropped by parachute into the wrong (we hoped) target area. On the emerald isle of Montserrat I was addressing my ball near the first green when the whole earth seemed to start shaking. A huge congregation (or whatever the noun of as-sembly is for such creatures) of landcrabs had decided to scurry back into the ground. But it was at this delightful twelve-hole course that I learned something of the international brotherhood of professional golf. A young islander who had hired out our clubs sold us half-a-dozen balls and, having seen us sign in suddenly appeared beside us on the first tee. 'Is there something wrong, pro?' I inquired, not wishing to be observed in yet another exhibition of incompetence off the tee. 'No, man.' he replied, 'I just come to see if you hit the ball as well as your son.' I stepped away from the address. 'How on earth do you know anything about my son?' I asked. 'Well, man,' came the answer. 'I read your name in the visitors' book and knew you was the English commentator with the England cricket team, 'cos I been listening to you. There's only one English commentator who has a son playing professional golf on the European circuit so it's easy to work out.' 'But what do you know about the European circuit?' I persisted. 'Have you been over there?' 'Lord, man, no,' he replied. 'I ain't never been nowhere outside this island, but I get the golf magazines and I keep up with what's happening over there.'

And he did – believe me – he did. There wasn't a player on the European circuit that young man didn't know about.

Perhaps my favourite memory of golfing abroad centres on the glorious Otago Golf Club course of Balmacewan, in Dunedin. It's easy to see why Scottish immigrants settled in such large numbers in this part of New Zealand's South Island. The city of Dunedin stands at the head of a long sea loch like Loch Linnhe or Loch Fyne; the main street is Princes Street, and parallel to it runs George Street. Districts are variously called St Kilda or Musselburgh, and the road from Dunedin to Central Otago passes through places named Dumbarton, Ettrick and Roxburgh. The Balmacewan course could have been transplanted from the Highlands of Scotland, especially when one considers the precipitous finishing hole where Chris Old, resting from his labours as an England fast bowler, had to pull my trolley as well as his own to the haven of the nineteenth. But it was on this sacred turf that I registered a birdie – an event in my golfing career as rare as a Ballesteros air-shot – with the help of a ricochet from a rock and a forty-foot putt. When I was told in the clubhouse, subsequently, that Jack Nicklaus had scored a birdie on that hole and it was, in fact, called the Nicklaus hole, my heart almost burst with joy. I should have retired from the game at that point and got out at the top.

And the most unpleasant memory? That would have to be
waking up in Kandy, high up in the hills of central Sri Lanka,
towards the end of the England cricket tour of 1981–2. A
colleague (Derek Hodgson, at that time of the *Daily Star*) came
in to break some disturbing news because he felt it would be
better than my reading it in the morning paper. An agency
report described how Ian and another golfer had been struck by
lightning while playing in the Vaal Reefs Open in South Africa.
It was only the barest couple of paragraphs and gave no
indication of whether Ian was injured or not. Naturally,
marooned thousands of miles away in another continent, one
fears the worst and all attempts to contact home (number
engaged, because my wife was making similar inquiries) or the
South African PGA in Johannesburg – which occupied my next
two hours – proved fruitless. Eventually, I asked my BBC
colleagues in London to find out what had happened and in less
than an hour they had called back to say that the boy had been
shaken but was otherwise unharmed because he had been
holding the wooden handle of his golf umbrella at the time. The
umbrella had, however, been plucked from his grasp and
hurled away. So that was the good news. The bad news, also
passed on during that same call from London, was that England's rugby captain, Bill Beaumont, had had to give up the
game because of a series of recent injuries.

By some way the best cricketer-golfer I have ever played with
is Neil Hawke, the Australian fast bowler who toured England
in 1964 and 1968, then, after a period as a Lancashire League
professional, settled in the town of Nelson and developed a
number of business interests in the North of England. 'Hawk-
eye' was a close friend of Fred Trueman, Peter Parfitt (the
former Middlesex and England batsman, who also settled in
the north after retirement from cricket) and myself, and, even
giving lots of shots off his handicap of one, he could usually beat
us comfortably. Hawke was a genial soul, a good companion
and a highly popular captain of Nelson Golf Club for a spell.
Tragically, a mind-boggling series of illnesses after his return to
South Australia saw him spend two years in hospital under-
going major surgery which left him without stomach muscles
and virtually without stomach. After something like a year in a

wheelchair he took his first tottering steps for over three years and immediately demanded to be taken to the nearest golf club to see if there was any immediate likelihood of taking up his golf where he had left off. His wife, Beverley, and his friends dissuaded him – for the moment – but they could not put off the day indefinitely. He finally stood once more on a practice ground and described the experience to me in a letter from Adelaide:

> I swung the club, and missed the ball by at least a foot. I swung again, and again, but couldn't make contact. My peace of mind was not helped by the sight of Beverley (in between pleas for me to pack it in and let her take me home) hitting a six-iron sweetly across the practice area. At last, after about an hour, it seemed, I finally made contact. The ball scuttled a few feet off the tee and two big tears rolled down my cheeks.

I have to say that two rolled down my cheeks as well as I read that. Can anyone imagine what it is like trying to play a golf shot on tottering legs, with no stomach muscles and just about a full set of plastic insides? And this was a huge, burly man who had been superbly fit and a very high-class amateur golfer as well as an Australian-Rules footballer. While at Nelson he did a great deal to help young players like Hogan Stott and to stimulate the growth of the club – one of my favourite people, Neil Hawke.

Topping the bill of cricketer-golfers in entertainment value comes the redoubtable F. S. Trueman, a unique character on the fairways where today he is seen with great frequency. It was not always so. In his playing days for Yorkshire and England, Fred believed in conserving all his energies for dealing with lesser mortals who dared to face him with a bat in their hands. After a day spent dismissing such creatures from his presence he liked to put his feet up. Similarly, at weekends he took the practical view that having laboured mightily for six days, he was not going to spend the seventh walking around three or four miles of parkland, heathland or sand dunes. But, whenever the subject was broached, he let it be known that if he *had* the inclination to join the golfers he had the ability to sort out the best of them, including Closey. In Fred's language, that meant 'especially Closey', but he rarely translated such threats into action. Except in the case of batsmen; with them he *always* kept his word.

After retiring from the first-class cricket scene, however, Fred's interest in golf developed and with it, his ability. When he started, he seemed to be able to hit the ball around 400 yards, but in no predictable direction, while his touch on the greens was some distance from being delicate. He was a difficult partner in a 'friendly' fourball since the amicable relationship would disappear with the first duff shot played by his mate. If, however, Fred strayed from line it was always attributable to factors entirely beyond his (or anyone's) control. FS has a fertile imagination and a round in his company is never less than hugely entertaining, though occasionally this involves a touch of masochism.

The arrival of the Celebrity Am–Am as a means of a raising money has been a major factor in stimulating even greater interest in the game amongst cricketers and, with it, Fred came into his own. His home is now a sort of Aladdin's Cave of prizes for success in Am–Ams: four sets of clubs, a cupboard full of Titleists and Dunlop 65s, silverware, glassware. And for the past three years he has run his own tournament, the Fred Trueman Classic, an extremely successful fund-raising day at the Oakdale Club in Harrogate. He has not yet contrived to win his own tournament, but don't discount the possibility. He has won just about everything else on that particular circuit.

Just where and when Fred received his tuition is something of a mystery, like his handicap. It is rumoured that the figure on the handicap board at El Paraiso, in Spain, where he plays a lot of winter golf with friends, differs considerably from that which appears on his card in British Am–Ams, an allegation which Fred simply denies without further elaboration or defence. With middle age has come a gentler approach to the game, and it is no longer possible to see quite so many putters hanging from trees on courses where he has recently jousted. But he has some strange theories, and club selection is not always the strongest part of his game.

1a The 1968 England Boys' team. *Back row (l. to r.):* Nigel Sumner, David Llewellyn, John Putt, Warren Humphreys, Ian Mosey, Ian Bamborough. *Front row:* Stephen Rooke, Nigel Sears, Steven Evans, A. W. P. White, Nick Rogers.

1b The 1972 England Youth team. *Back row (l. to r.):* David J. Russell, Bob Larratt, Andrew Chandler, Martin Foster, Howard Clark, Pip Elson, Ken Saint. *Front row:* Peter Berry, John Putt, Ian Mosey, Roger Revell, Carl Mason.

2 Tony Jacklin and Ian Mosey after Ian's win in a sudden-death play-off for the Merseyside International Open Championship in 1980.

3a Ian Woosnam gets out of trouble in the 1987 World Match-Play tournament at Wentworth.

3b Bernhard Langer: the dreaded yips strike again (1986 French Open).

4a Greg Norman: 'a cocoon of concentration' (1986 World Match-Play tournament at Wentworth).

4b Seve Ballesteros – and his gallery – demand the ball to drop (1988 Open at Royal Lytham).

5a Another moment of triumph for Nick Faldo.

5b Sandy Lyle's war dance as his putt goes in to win the 1988 Masters' in Augusta.

6a 'The fisherman dropped Brian on a deserted beach in northern Sardinia.'
(p. 59)

6b 'Charlie – a very large crocodile who normally sleeps soundly beside the
pond with a fine disregard for all golfing activity taking place round about
him.' (p. 94)

7a 'Hobday put on a Viking helmet, horns and all, and holed the shot. How the crowd loved it.' (p. 129)

7b 'The tractor-driver continued on his way, towing a trailer and a senior BBC engineer, leaving Chris and Mrs Jacqui Newton gazing at each other in a state of near hysteria.' (p. 143)

8a The first and eighteenth holes and the world headquarters of golf: the Royal and Ancient Golf Club of St Andrews.

8b 'The fiddling little course' of Mont Agel, home of the Monte Carlo Open.

When we operated together in Tests in London it was our pleasure to stay with friends Claude and Morag Brownlow at their home in Tiptree (Essex) during the weekend. The house-party usually consisted of the late Maharajah of Baroda (who sadly died in 1988), Fred and his wife Veronica, my wife Jo and myself and, of course, our hosts. On Sunday mornings, while 'Jackie' Baroda ranged the girls about him beside the swimming pool in the style of handmaidens, Fred, Claude and I took ourselves off to Colchester golf club to make up a four with one of Claude's business partners, an Australian called Greg. Fred affected a natural, professional hatred of all Aussies (while proclaiming, with his next breath, his undying friendship with men like Ray Lindwall, Alan Davidson and Neil Harvey). Greg was, easily and naturally, a born *agent provocateur*. From the first tee we were on a collision course on the first of these encounters. After only one hole, Greg wandered across and casually inquired, 'What will you bet that I can't talk Fred into playing the wrong club?' After two losing bets I abandoned my part in such wagers; Greg did not so much *talk* Fred into over-clubbing as *goad* him into it. It was a noisy fourball which made its way around the course, and on the eighteenth tee (it was, in fact, the ninth because Sunday morning congestion had led us to start at the tenth) Fred and I were one down. Claude went wildly left and we were to see no more of him until we reached the green; I pushed my tee shot out to the right, and before I had any sort of view of the green I had to chip out sideways and then a seven-iron put me on the green for three. Fred, ten yards ahead, weighed up his next move and Greg sidled over to ask, 'How about a nominal 10p that I can't make him use a wood?'

Well, I might as well recoup two bob of the money I had lost already and we looked like losing the match in any case. It was a safe bet, No way in the world was Fred going to take wood for a shot of 130 yards. Honour demanded I say nothing as Greg eased his way to my partner's side. My blood ran cold as I saw Fred start to take out a club, hesitate, then exchange it. He then addressed the ball and smote it – with a wooden club. The ball soared over the green, over a fence, over a house and garden; we were playing Colchester and the ball was last seen approaching Southend. Fred followed its flight for one moment of horrified silence; Greg collapsed on to the ground in a paroxysm of hysterical laughter and with the prospect of losing several quid as well as my two bob, and the rest, now looming large, I snarled at Fred, 'What the hell did you use?'

'A —— three-wood,' replied my partner, in a state of apoplexy. 'I was going to use my four so I could stop it on the green but this Aussie —— said it needed a three.'

'But Fred,' I protested, 'I've just got there with a seven-iron and I played from ten yards behind you.'

After years of experience I should have known better. No one ever has the last word with FST. 'A seven?' he said, fine contempt mixed with apparent disbelief at such folly. 'A seven? Well, *you* used the wrong —— club, sunshine.'

To this day he blames me for the two-hole defeat.

Don: Your fourth year on the circuit, 1976, brought a bit of success and you finished forty-ninth in the European Order of Merit. Would you describe that as a turning point in your professional career?

Ian: Not really. It was more like a one-off year because I couldn't seem to achieve any degree of consistency. In 1974, I had won the Lancashire Under-23 Championship at Leigh and the Lancashire Open Championship at St Anne's Old, and I played in the Open at Royal Lytham that year when a sixteen-year-old schoolboy listed in the programme as Mr A. W. B. Lyle got through to the third day. Little did we realise how much we were going to hear of that young man in the future. The following year (1975) was the first time the Greater Manchester Open was staged, and I badly wanted to win it. Most of my success had been fairly local (although I had picked up a few hundred pounds on the Safari Circuit in Nigeria a year earlier) and I looked at the Greater Manchester as *my* tournament. I prepared really hard for it and I was determined to score my first win amongst most of the big names in the country in that one. I led after the first round, then the second. On the third morning I went to practise at Denton for a late tee-ing off time at Wilmslow, and that's where I made a terrible mistake.

I left myself an hour to get from Denton to Wilmslow, which was more than enough in normal circumstances, but what I completely overlooked was (a) that they are all two-car families in Wilmslow and every vehicle in the town is on the road on Saturday morning, and (b) that it was the day of the Woodford Air Show and so the normal heavy volume of traffic had multiplied by four. I was late on the tee, penalised two strokes and started out in a savage fury as well as a state of mental unpreparedness. I really threw that one away and instead of banking my first big cheque I ended the season with total

earnings of £341 for five months of hard slog and a lot of
expense. I needed to do something dramatically better in 1976
or it would be necessary to find another way of earning a living.

Don: The Open was at Royal Birkdale that year and it
coincided with the Old Trafford Test Match in a season in
which we saw the emergence of the West Indies as the most
potent force in world cricket. I missed that Test to produce the
Open golf coverage at Southport and nipped out of our Radio 2
caravan to watch Ian come through the ninth hole on the
Friday afternoon. As ever, I had to conceal myself furtively in
the crowd and, as ever, my stomach churned horribly as my son
weighed up a birdie putt on the green. I was just breathing a
prayer of thanks as the putt went in when a voice spoke quietly
into my ear: 'You must be very proud of the boy.' Sir Leonard
Hutton, hero of my childhood, friend of my adult years, has
always been a golf enthusiast and has taken a distant, avuncu-
lar kind of interest in Ian throughout his career. Now he had
forsaken the Test match to come and watch some golf. Twelve
years later, amidst the massive celebrations to mark the fiftieth
anniversary of his 364 runs against Australia at the Oval, Sir
Leonard was at the Headingley Test amongst the huge crowd of
well-wishers in the pavilion when he encountered my wife. 'Ian
did a 68 yesterday,' he said to her. 'Give him my congratulations, won't you?' One of the nicest aspects of my working life
has been the number of cricketing friends who take an interest
in the boy's golf. Just occasionally this can be a trifle obtrusive.

In 1985, during cricket commentary at Old Trafford with
Freddie Trueman as my summariser, I noticed out of the corner
of my eye that FS had been slipped a note by the producer and
was clearly in a state of some excitement as he waited for the
end of the over so he could make an announcement. He then
proclaimed triumphantly, 'In the Scandinavian Open golf
championship, Ian Mosey has had a hole in one and it's won
him an £11,000 Saab car.' Now what, I ask you, does a father
say to that – in the middle of a cricket commentary? An ace is
generally regarded as a bit of a fluke, an acceptable sort of
accident for sure, but not something to shoot a line about by any
means. I muttered something like, 'Well done' or 'Congratulations to him', and turned Fred's attention back to the cricket.

But within a couple of minutes Ray Illingworth, from the TV commentary box next door (another old friend, a Saab driver and a man with a keen eye for a bargain) was round to see me. 'Do you think Ian will bring the car back with him?' he inquired, speculatively.

Ian: I didn't, of course. I exchanged it for cash on the spot and with a feeling of some relief. That hole in one – a four-iron at the 187-yard fifth hole – probably saved my bacon because I was playing rubbish at the time and looked like missing the cut. But all this was a long way in the future as I struggled through the lean years of the mid-seventies. Four days of the 1976 Open at Birkdale won me £238, and as I picked up a bit of money in the Benson and Hedges and the Irish Open it proved my most successful year so far. The important thing was that I had won a total of £3,178 in more distinguished company than usual, and I hoped that I had turned the corner and that things would start to go well from that point. In 1977 and 1978, however, everything went wrong again and I was now in something like despair. I was questioning my ability to exist at this level of golf. Something had gone seriously wrong with my game and there was no Brian Allen to turn to. My friends on the circuit could help to iron out minor wrinkles but I was convinced that only Brian could make any major adjustments which were necessary, and he was now beyond my reach. I was in my twenty-eighth year at the start of the 1979 season and not making anything like a living wage. At this point, those relatives who had asked, 'When is Ian going to get a job?' might well have put the question again with great pertinence.

All kinds of other questions were now also relevant. Was my game good enough? If not, what was wrong with it? Was it possible to put things right? Was I *thinking* my way round a golf course correctly? If not, why not? Once personal confidence begins to seep away, golf becomes a very tough game indeed and common sense dictated that after six years of solid competition at the highest level I ought to be playing with more confidence than I now felt. From the wonderful feeling of being in the top fifty in 1976 I now looked back on a couple of years in which I slumped to 84th in 1977 and 116th in 1978. One moment found me reflecting soberly that the time had come to

say, 'Enough', and to accept that I was simply not good enough
to carry on the fight; the next I was remembering all those hours
of practice on Heartbreak Hill and asking if they had all
been for nothing. I thought of all the time that Brian Allen had
spent with me (out of his own pocket, so to speak) and of his
encouragement and his faith in my ability to make it as a pro. I
thought of the other people who helped along the way. Towards
the end of the 1978 season I was not even giving myself a chance
of winning money, so confused was my mind and so depressed
my spirits.

If it had not been for a reasonable amount of success in South
Africa, where I was now a regular visitor, it would simply not
have been possible for me to continue on the European circuit.
But I needed to make money in the European summer to
finance my visits to South Africa. I was caught in a particularly
vicious financial circle. Thank God it was at this time that I
discovered John Jacobs, initially through a TV series of golf
instruction and then through reading his commonsense views
on the game. But it was still make-or-break time when I set off
for the Sunshine Circuit (which usually seems to start with rain
and wind!) in 1978–9. Fourth place in the Victoria Falls Classic
gave me the best possible encouragement, especially with a
record-equalling first round of 68, five under par on the longest
course in Africa at 7,868 yards, which was playing even longer
than that after a week of heavy rain. One newspaper reported
that I had brought my own weather with me from Manchester,
but the truth is that my putter got me round on the first day. I
used it just twenty-eight times and led a major tournament for
the first time in my life. Inevitably, it seemed, I followed this
with a 75, but that might have been a lot worse.

At the turn I was five over par as a result of one or two
adventures, notably at the short eighth, where I put my tee shot
into Charlie's Pond. Charlie is a renowned figure at Elephant
Hills – a very large crocodile who normally sleeps soundly
beside the pond with a fine disregard for all golfing activity
taking place round about him. On this occasion he might have
been away visiting relatives. On the other hand he might just as
easily have been lurking in the depths of the pond, and I have
an inherited family horror of all things reptilian. If I had been

playing better I would have taken a drop, but the round was assuming disastrous proportions at that time and I could see the ball lying close to the edge of the water. Golfing ambition overcame physical terror; I took off shoes and socks and played my ball out of the pond and on to the green. Charlie, mercifully, never appeared and though I still two-putted, I came back in 33 to achieve some sort of respectability. Third place in the South African Open behind Hugh Baiocchi and Gavin Levenson helped me to end the tour as leading Briton in the Order of Merit and to start 1979 at home in a very much more settled state of mind. I won the Lancashire Open for the third time but, more to the point, improved my European Order of Merit position from 116th in 1978 to 69th. Earnings in Europe of £3,357 just about covered the outgoings and made it possible to tackle the Sunshine Circuit again.

We must not, however, leave the winter of 1978–9 without a story which illustrates the luck of the Irish, or perhaps the persistence of that nation. Standing on the first tee at Elephant Hills at the start of a practice round, Roddy Carr heard a telephone ringing. As one does, automatically, he looked round to see where a telephone might be located in those wide open spaces and found it was a temporary installation underneath the starter's table. As the official picked up the phone, Roddy turned away with no further interest in the call until he heard the shout, 'Telephone for Mr Carr. It's a long-distance call from Dublin.' Disbelievingly, Roddy took up the phone to find that it was a relative calling from home. 'How did you know I was here?' he asked. Then, looking across the Zambezi river to distant Zambia, he inquired, 'Where am I, anyway?' Ah, the whimsical Irish . . .

Don: Ian has been a regular visitor to South Africa for the past fifteen winters. In some quarters that may be regarded as reprehensible. In others, not so vocal but none the less sincere for that, it will be approved and even applauded. Golf is not the only game which attracts sportsmen to a beautiful country with a congenial climate. But this is not intended to be a book with any political overtones or undertones of any kind. Ian first went to South Africa because it seemed a good place to follow his profession during the English winter. He has continued to go because he enjoys playing there, and because the people of that country have been good to him – just how good is indicated in some of the following pages.

Ian: On my arrival for the first time in South Africa, for the winter of 1975–6, I had a one-way ticket, a travel voucher which I hoped would get me home in due course, and £20 in my pocket. As I was planning to be there for at least a couple of months, I was nothing if not optimistic! From the telephone directory I learned that the address of the South African PGA was 'Loveday Street, Johannesburg', which is in the centre of the city. With clubs and clothing for an extended stay, I tramped virtually the length of Loveday Street when I found it, and it seemed about ten miles long. Eventually I found a tiny office which dealt with the club professional side of golf in South Africa and also housed the Amateur Football Association. It wasn't the place I wanted at all. However, the officials there directed me to the Wanderers Club. Here I met Brian Henning, one of four brothers who were such a dominating force in South African golf at that time. He was not overwhelmingly enthusiastic, and I didn't blame him for that; the arrival of I. J. Mosey was not going to enhance the quality of the tournament scene very much at all. But he directed me to the Sands Hotel with the advice that I would find a pronounced golfing ambience. This was absolutely right. The proprietor, Abie Katz, was a keen golfer himself and enjoyed having professionals staying with him. The Wanderers, however, was some distance away and daily taxi fares to go and practise just about broke my heart and my bank balance.

Don: There can't have been much left of your £20 after the first week.

Ian: That's right. The hotel cost me a flat rate of about £10, and for that I got two meals a day. I had not much money in my pocket, true, but I didn't look further ahead in those days than the end of the week. Something would turn up. Inevitably, I got into conversation with a group of chaps at the Wanderers and the usual questions were asked: 'Are you playing the tour over here? Where are you staying?' Amongst the group was a man called Larry Akema, who immediately said, 'You don't want to stay in a hotel in the middle of town. Come and stay with me.'

Just like that, to a complete stranger from overseas. So there and then, that very evening, he took me home with him. He had a beautiful home and a lovely, motherly type of wife, and he lived about five minutes from the course. On the first morning I went to the course and practised, then returned for lunch and decided to have an hour in the swimming pool. In the middle of summer at midday in Johannesburg! The next morning my shoulders were burned to a crisp and I felt very tight across the top of my arms. Nevertheless, I went out to practise and the morning after that I was in complete agony.

Don: You really weren't fit to be allowed out without your mother to keep on eye on you, were you?

Ian: Well, you learn these things the hard way, don't you? Anyway, the blisters 'popped' and, true to form with me, within a day it had all gone septic. I was in a terrible state and my first tournament in South Africa was coming up in a week's time. My shoulders were raw and my arms virtually wouldn't function. Larry, a good golfer who took the game very seriously, was not too impressed with his house-guest. Not so his wife, thank goodness. She now enlisted the aid of her best friend in applying the only remedy for my affliction – poultices which had to be applied, and changed, around the clock. And this is what they did: a lady I had met for the first time only a couple of days earlier and her friend who didn't know me at all. They fought the blood-poisoning, which had set in as well, and worked twenty-four hours a day to keep my chest and shoulders swathed in fresh bandages – wonderful people.

Amazingly, I was in some sort of shape for the tournament and started with four consecutive birdies and won a cheque by the end of it. Larry then had a change of heart, realising perhaps that I was a stupid youngster rather than an irresponsible playboy, and I stayed with him for quite a while. On the way back from a tournament in Swaziland I met a couple called Neil and Ros Fuller, with whom I stayed for the remainder of that season and the whole of the next one. That is another friendship which has endured, and I shall never forget what I owe to the Akemas and the Fullers. Later I met John Burnett at the Wanderers, the focal centre of things on the South African tour, and I have stayed with John and his wife for the past six years. Happily, I am now able to reciprocate, and he stays with me when he comes over to the Open, and I can do something for his children when they visit this country.

Don: What about caddies in South Africa?

Ian: I have had only two since I started playing over there in 1975. The first was called Johannes, who was keen to play and wanted to become a pro himself. I gave him equipment and lessons and I used to sneak him on to the courses in Johannesburg on Mondays (when they are all closed for maintenance) and tried to encourage him. Then he went out of golf and since 1981 I have had a caddy called Stanley, who is quiet and doesn't aspire to being a player himself. Over the past six or seven years we have formed what I think is quite a good team. All the caddies are black and Stanley does the job all the year round. In recent years the caddies have developed upon European tour lines and there is a group of full-time tournament operators who get pretty reasonably paid. I pay Stanley 250 rand a week and 5 per cent of prize money so he has a regular wage and quite a few bonuses. He also enjoys the kudos of being a well-known TV caddy because I get featured quite a lot on the small screen and that helps him get work in the remainder of the year. By travelling with me he gets to see the whole of his country, which not everyone, black or white, has done in a huge place like South Africa.

I was able to give him a bit of help of the sort which European caddies do not often have to ask for. He and his girlfriend had a baby four years ago and Stanley wanted to marry her and set up a home. But while it was all right for them to have the child, they could not marry until Stanley had conformed with tribal custom by paying her father a bride-price. Traditionally, this used to be payable in cattle but nowadays cash is acceptable. Stanley had been saving for years but still hadn't got the required amount and during the 1987–8 season I increased his percentage and advanced him 1,000 rand against future earnings. Happily, I was runner-up in the South African Open shortly afterwards, and with a string of top-ten finishes Stanley was able to pay off the advance quite quickly. This enabled them to get married, and for the first time he could live with the lady and their child, who previously had to stay, along with his mother, at her parents' home. There is no objection to what in Europe would be known as promiscuity as long as the couple do not actually live together, so I hope they live happily ever after – and that I have not damaged the structure of tribal tradition. Stanley keeps in touch with me through the Burnetts and I look forward to renewing our partnership each winter.

In 1980, which was when my career in South Africa really took off – although I didn't know that it was going to – I stayed with a character called Jan Slootweg, a real Dutchman from Amsterdam, who was not a very good golfer but was a re-nowned gambler at the game in his own club at Glendower. He and his wife were a middle-aged, childless couple, who lived on the edge of the course. Financially and physically it was probably the best tour I have ever undertaken: financially because it was the year I was runner-up in the South African Open for the first time and I had a string of other good finishes; physically because of the home-cooking at the Slootweg's home.

In dietary terms I had come a long way since that first winter in Spain and I now ate *everything*. The Slootwegs grew their own vegetables and there were at least three varieties with a meat dish every evening for dinner. They introduced me to endives, rich in vitamins, and I ate piles of them with the result that I took an inch and a half off my waistline but put a lot of muscle on elsewhere. When I was not playing tournament golf, I played social stuff with Jan for a nominal 20 rand, but within the club he had on-going competitions with just about every other member. I once calculated his turnover in bets at a minimum of 8,000 rand a week – mostly losing bets! He had a regular four-ball against the two guys who ran the sports shop at Glendower, and they coined thousands from Jan because he never seemed to have a partner who could help him. Then he started taking me, with a four-figure sum on the match, and because they had been taking Jan for so long (and wanted to do so again when I had gone back to England) they couldn't say 'No' to his new partner. They started to lose and they really hated it. Just the same, we slipped up on one notable occasion when Jan got carried away and challenged John Bland and a renowned gambler, Wally Pienaar, from ERPM golf club. John is a very good tournament player indeed, but he plays even better 'for fun' than he does on the circuit and he shot a 64 which cost Jan five grand.

No tribute to my many good friends in South Africa would be complete without mention of 'Uncle George' Blumberg, who was a benefactor to so many sportsmen (including just about every black golfer), without fuss or ostentation, and certainly without publicity. I first met him in my amateur days at Newcastle, Co. Down, where he was supporting a good amateur he had brought over to play in the 1970 British Amateur Championship, Kevin Sullivan. I was drawn to play Joe Carr in the second round, but Kevin beat Joe in the first and so the modest gallery for my second-round match included Uncle George and his wife, Brenda. I was carrying my pencil bag, as usual, and wearing rubber Stylo shoes in the middle of summer – the perfect picture of an impoverished young player. I beat Sullivan and Uncle George approached me afterwards to ask, 'Do you never have a caddy?' 'No,' I replied, 'it's a luxury I just cannot afford.' He then asked if I was going to play in The Open and I said I was hoping to.

'Right,' said Uncle George. 'If you pre-qualify at St Andrews, you find me and I'll make sure you have a caddy.' Not knowing Mr Blumberg at the time, I didn't really take the offer seriously and in any case I was so overwhelmed by the thought of playing in The Open for the first time that I didn't think any more about it. I was in the locker-room at the home of world golf, rubbing shoulders with men who were just names in the newspapers to me and generally in seventh heaven when Uncle George walked in. *He* had found *me*. He said, 'Congratulations' and put two £20 notes in my hand. My first reaction was one of horror – or perhaps terror is a better word. There I was at St Andrews, an amateur, about to play in The Open, and someone had given me *money*. Had I surrendered my amateur status? Hoping that no one had seen, I crept into a corner and looked at the notes. I had never seen a £20 note in my life and now I had two of them. So I could pay for a caddy and, as I did not make the third-round cut, I had change from one of the notes and the other was still intact. I searched for Uncle George to return it but I couldn't find him anywhere. I

carried that £20 note with me for the rest of the year. I simply
could not bring myself to spend it. It was like that Cary Grant
film where he was given a million-pound note and simply on its
credit strength could buy anything he wanted. That's how I felt
about my twenty-pounder. To me it was the equivalent of a
million.

When I started going to South Africa I never looked Uncle
George up. Dropping hints and hoping for a bed for the night
was part of our way of life and it did not seem terribly
reprehensible. But chasing up a man who handed out cash was
another matter altogether and I steered clear. However, the
thing that makes all the difference to one's quality of life on tour
is being independent as far as transport is concerned – in other
words, having a car. It was Noel Hunt who said to me, after
three years of the Sunshine Circuit without wheels, 'Why don't
you contact Uncle George? He'll lend you one.' So I wrote to
him before I set out again and he replied, 'Come and see me and
we'll see what we can do.' So I went to see him – he had a big
papermill in the southern suburbs of Johannesburg where he
kept a collection of old cars. It wasn't as if he needed them;
somehow he just could not bear to part with them. He had a
Mark IX Jaguar, the one with the big front that looked like a
Bentley, a black one, a huge thing, a monster. And he had an
old American car from the 1950s with fins and about thirty
lights on it, and an assortment of old bangers as well.

I was lent the American job for the duration of the tour and
very quickly learned that it not only had power-steering but
power-everything-else as well. I was going down a narrow
street to have some trousers altered at a tailor's shop and I
switched off seconds too early. The steering locked, as did the
brakes, and I had a nasty moment before bringing it to a stop.
The following year I got another monster which had an alarm
which went off all the time. It was all adventure. Uncle George,
generous soul that he was, loaned various cars from his collection to a variety of golfers and I yearned for the moment when I
could get my hands on the Jaguar. Nicky Price had it the first
year, Warren Humphreys the second and eventually my turn
came – at the very moment when sanctions against South
Africa were biting. The price of petrol went through the roof

and the Jag did about three miles to the gallon! Sadly, the car was broken into while I was staying in a flat in Hillbrow, Johannesburg and the parts which were stolen were irreplaceable.

But Uncle George uttered no word of reproach. He always helped when any of us needed help – Dale Hayes, Bobby Cole and Gary Player himself in his early days – as well as those of us from overseas. He was a wonderful, lovable, generous man who never sought or expected thanks, and certainly not public acknowledgement, of his many benefactions.

9 Some You Win, Some You Don't

Ian: If I have established any sort of international reputation at all it is probably as the golfer who 'choked' on the last green in the South African Open of 1979. It is a reputation I would rather be without, especially as I feel the description is just a little inaccurate. But 'choking' to one man is something quite different to another and the headlines back in England on that weekend in December 1979 reached a fairly unanimous conclusion: 'Mosey Muffs Last Hole and Top Prize', 'Disaster at Eighteenth for Ian', 'Open Title Handed to Player'. Were they strictly accurate?

Don: Well, writers have to describe a situation as *they* see it and headline-writers take their lead from the copy before them. There can be little doubt that the agency reporters in Johannesburg who saw your disaster interpreted it as being due to 'choking' – in other words, finding the tension of the situation just a bit too much for you. To someone who had not discussed the precise details of your final round with you it must certainly have looked that way. We shall look at it from your angle in a moment, but first may I describe that final day from the point of view of a parent, biting his nails through the afternoon, 5,000 miles away?

I was due to broadcast the Rugby Union County Championship semi-final between Surrey and Lancashire from the London Welsh ground in Richmond and the BBC Radio Sports Unit, aware that Ian was starting the final round with a two-stroke lead at the head of the field, arranged to 'hook me up' for a conversation with my son on the air in 'Sports Report' if he won the tournament. In the event, the producer forgot all about this when, in fact, Ian did not win, and left one frantic father at the Outside Broadcast point in Richmond without any information about what was happening in Johannesburg! They had got my last report on the Rugby match and when the news came from South Africa that Gary Player had won the Open, D.

Mosey's services were no longer required that day. I could not
'raise' the studio and the people there were not disposed to call
me. It was only when I got back to my hotel and directed an
extremely disgruntled inquiry to Broadcasting House that I
learned Ian had been runner-up. So what exactly happened?

Ian: The previous winter I had finished in third place in the
South African Open by holing a long putt on the seventeenth
and a huge one on the eighteenth. It was in all truth a rather
sneaky way to get into the top three.

In 1979, by contrast, it all went rather differently. They had
hemmed the fairways in tight and it was a straight-hitter's
course at Houghton. I remember Alan Henning, one of South
Africa's senior golfers, saying that it was a good, tight course
and there would be no surprise winner of the Open after I had
done a first-round 68 to put me one behind Gary Player. I had a
sort of feeling that he might have been thinking of me when he
said it and this remained with me for the rest of the week; it
spurred me on a little bit. I played pretty solidly and I had a
game plan for the course. I had just begun to learn something
about 'managing' a course, and with lots of right-to-left holes
Houghton suited my game. A second round of 70 gave me a one-
stroke lead over the field and 69 in the third increased my lead to
two strokes over Simon Hobday. Player was now six shots behind me as we went into the final eighteen holes. He was, however, playing in front of me – and he birdied the first four holes!

Gary was, of course, famous for that sort of charge and for
producing miracles at the right time, so he took most of the
crowd with him. By the time he had holed his fourth birdie he
had *the whole* of the crowd with him and there I was, the
tournament leader and therefore last out, trailing along with no
one watching me. I have experienced this several times in my
life and it sows the seeds of doubt in one's mind; it creates an
impression that it's all slipping away from you. By the sixth
hole he had drawn level with me and I was then in a very
competitive situation; it was like match-play against a man I
could not even see, but strangely enough, though I could not for
the life of me have explained why, I found myself enjoying it. I
birdied the seventh, making a good four from a bunker, and
Gary had a par-five, up ahead of me. The bunker was a bit bare

and really it was a shot where I should have tried to play safe by aiming away from the flag. But I got up and down in two and I remember thinking with some pleasure that I was making a good job of *competing* with the great man. So I stayed one ahead up to the fourteenth, another par-five, where my thinking went a bit wrong. I hit a fairway driver for my second to the front edge of the green and so I had two putts for my birdie. With hindsight, it was the wrong shot to play at that time. If I had used a one-iron and left myself with a straightforward short pitch and finished the hole by numbers, it would have been wiser.

Now I had put pressure on myself by straying from the orthodox, at least in terms of the way I had planned the round, and I started to feel a few flutters. Anyway, I three-putted, but it was still a par-five. No great harm done, but suddenly I was aware that I was playing at an artificially elevated level. I started to think about the possibility of winning instead of playing each hole, and each shot, as it came. On fifteen and sixteen I made good, solid par-fours and the seventeenth is a par-three, up-hill and over water – only about a seven-iron but in avoiding the water I hit it too far. Now, the greens had a lot of grain to them and as the seventeenth was a patchwork green there was no way to read it. Having chipped back too far, I had about a seven-footer to stay one up and one to play. Whenever I think about the stories of my 'choking' I think of that putt. It was a left-to-right slope and a left-to-right grain and the putt had to be firm and brave. I made it. So when I am reminded of how I 'threw the South African Open away' I think of the shots like that – shots that I had to make simply to stay in contention during the week.

So, with Player finishing with a last-round 66, I stood on the eighteenth tee needing a par-four to win my first tournament after seven years on the circuit. It's an excellent finishing hole, 420 yards, a little uphill with a slight dogleg, right to left. I was very much aware of the situation, playing with Alan Henning and Simon Hobday, but I felt quite in control of it – no more flutters, no nervousness. I was a pro with a professional job to do and I concerned myself simply with doing it properly. And then, right at the top of my backswing, when I was completely committed to the stroke, a butterfly settled on my ball and

attracted my attention, of course. I swung very fast played a
duck-hook and with the hole going right to left I put myself in
the wrong spot, and amongst the television cables as well.
However, I was on bare ground under some trees and the shot
to the green was 'on'. But my two partners were in similar
trouble – both needed rulings – and it took a long time to clear
the cables for the three of us to play our next shots. In fact, it
took *half an hour* to play the hole. I could have done without that
then, because with Player in the clubhouse after his 66, he had
set the target and now I was very much the centre of media
attention. When you have been in that position scores of times it
may be different, but I was experiencing it for the first time.
And it was now that I made an error of strategy.

The green is long and narrow, so I didn't want to miss it. I
could have played just short and pitched the ball down the
green with every expectation of getting close. But the pin was
rather tight on the left and as my natural shot is right to left I
went for it, overdid the draw and missed the green on the left –
exactly where I did not want to be. That left me with a pitch, no
room to work with and off a very tight lie. I carried three wedges
in my bag in those days, one of them an old Spalding with a
sharp edge, so it was very much a 'touch' club. These days we
have clubs with square grooves and big soles and they are really
pressure-proof clubs, but this was a very light, thin-bladed 'feel'
wedge and I felt happy with it. I opened it as much as I dared
and hit the highest, softest possible shot, which was a beauty.
Now, if ever I was going to choke it was on that pitch under
more pressure than I had ever known in my life, and I played it
as well as I possibly could have done, to about fifteen feet.

By now I was really stimulated, completely charged up. It
was like one of those games you play as a child – 'I've got this
putt to win the South African Open' – only this wasn't a child's
game. It was real, very real. The putt was slightly uphill and it
'went' about two inches from right to left, with the grain right to
left as well, and in South Africa if you don't play for the grain
the ball gets 'buried'. So I hit it very hard and very 'high' – it
was the right sort of bad putt. And it went straight over the top
of the hole, stopping about fifteen to eighteen inches beyond it.
But that didn't mean anything to me. My first putt had not

gone in and I had *not* won the South African Open. That was all
I could think about. The thought that I had the return putt to
square the tournament with Gary Player on ten-under-par and
go into a play-off never occurred to me. All I could think was
that I had had one putt to win and I hadn't made it. If I had just
quit on the putt, even slightly, the grain would have hit it and
the ball would have gone in. But I had been too firm and I had
lost my chance. No thought of a play-off crossed my mind; quite
simply, I had not won and that was it. I was utterly deflated. I
didn't line up the second putt at all. I didn't mark it (which we
do to keep the 'label' in the same place all the time; it's a little
exercise in discipline which helps you under pressure). I didn't
do any of that because the putt had no significance to me at all.
And I missed.

I had left myself with a putt, with left-to-right grain, from
about eighteen inches on a flat-looking green – the most
terrifying putt of all. Psychologically, it is very difficult to hit the
ball firmly on the left lip when it *looks* flat. I know from experience that you must do it but everything was going to be against
me if I played it without preparation and without much thought.
I just wandered up to the ball and dribbled it and it died under
the hole. I still wasn't thinking about a play-off; I had simply
lost my chance of a title and a winner's cheque. The importance
of the putt was recognised by everyone else, however, and it
was prime time TV on the only channel which existed at that
time so everyone in the country saw it. Interestingly, in view
of the 'choking' and 'muffing' descriptions which were applied
at the time, the public in South Africa reacted with tremendous
sympathy and, ten years later, the significance of the missed
putt(s) still evokes the same response from the public there.

Don: Of all the comments I read on that experience – and
there was a lot of reading to be done that week! – one of the most
understanding came in an article by Donald Steel in the
following weekend's *Sunday Telegraph*:

Last week's experience of Ian Mosey in the South African
Open was a further example of how cruel golf can be.
Mosey had played three excellent rounds, preserved his
lead on the final day with great resolution in difficult

circumstances, and stood on the 72nd tee in Johannesburg needing a four to emulate Tommy Horton, the only British golfer to win the South African Open.

Victory would have been the sure sign that years of struggle had been worthwhile. It is not always appreciated that professional golf is a lonely, hard life for the vast majority and that periodic success is necessary in keeping despair at arm's length. Dreams can quickly fade but the fact that Mosey, 69th in this year's Order of Merit, was quoted as saying he didn't really remember anything about taking three putts for the six which left him in second place underlines the plight of golfers in such a situation.

What a contrast to Gary Player, winner for the twelfth time and one of the game's greatest golfers, finding himself six strokes behind and then cruising round in 66. No real pressure – over 100 victories behind him, two of them in the previous two weeks.

If, for once, he had taken 68, what a difference it would have made to Mosey, although, despite the opportunity that was there, Mosey's performance deserved the utmost praise. It was far better than anything he has yet approached and, with the right philosophical acceptance of what has happened, it should act as a spur . . . Mosey's efforts should encourage all those launched, or embarking, on a tournament career that faith and perseverance are essential qualities which do have their reward.

So that was one tournament that got away. In September the following year there came, at last, one which didn't.

Ian: The Merseyside International Open was staged, for the first and only time, at Hoylake (Royal Liverpool GC) in 1980 and the south-west wind rose in high fury to welcome it. It was the week of the Hennessey Cup, so a lot of the major stars weren't there, but Tony Jacklin *was*. However, mine was still an also-ran sort of name and I got a place in the pro–am, before the tournament itself, as a bit of an afterthought on the part of the organisers. Consequently, I went out in the first four, with John Morgan behind me on a perfect morning. I shot 73, John 77 – and no one else broke 80. As I stood on the eleventh (the Alps), the wind started to blow, an offshoot of a hurricane out in the Atlantic, and some of the finishing holes became unplayable. My team won and so to start the week I had found a nice little earner in a pro–am in which I had not expected to play. In the tournament itself – scheduled as a fifty-four-hole competition – we started in extremely difficult conditions and I shot 72.

In the second round I had a late starting-time and Warren Humphreys, who was staying with me in Manchester, had an early start. He went off after breakfast and phoned me in the middle of the morning to say, 'Don't bother to set off. It looks as though we are not going to play.' I looked out of the window and it was a brilliantly sunny morning in Manchester. Although Warren had said he would ring again to warn me if play was going to start, I just dared not sit at home past my scheduled starting time (remembering, perhaps, the disaster of that first Greater Manchester Open). So I drove over to the Wirral and, on the side of the first fairway, close to the putting green, I saw Mike King hitting practice balls into the wind with his sand-iron, watching them come back over his head, land on the putting green and bounce against the clubhouse wall. In all the time I have been playing, it was the only time I have known a day's tournament play called off because of wind – as that one was. So with Friday cancelled, we had to play two rounds on Saturday.

Warren was closely in contention going into the second round but his challenge began to drift away. Jacklin was very much the class player in the field, and we were all conscious of him, but I was young and fit and I liked thirty-six holes in a day; I began to feel good as we started the third round, still in extremely windy conditions, but not bad enough for play to be called off. The first hole was virtually unplayable, with the wind carrying second shots into the out-of-bounds area; holes like fourteen and sixteen were playing short but there was no way to stop the ball. It was very difficult indeed.

It wasn't a tournament with lots of leader-boards and one didn't really know what was happening to the rest of the field, so I just tried to keep it going in a workmanlike sort of way. At the short thirteenth I caught a glimpse of a board at last. It showed me either one or two strokes behind Jacklin, who had not quite finished his round and on fourteen I hit the ball into the wrong place. For the first time I was carrying a five-wood in my bag, almost as if I had the next shot in mind. It was straight down-wind and I wanted something I could pop straight in the air; it paid off – I knocked it on and made a birdie four. I birdied sixteen with the help of a good putt, and seventeen, a famous hole indeed, was so far out of range that I had to play a six-iron for my *third* at a par-four! I stood on the last tee of a hole I remembered from the 1972 Brabazon, knowing I needed a three to tie with Tony so I took an iron off the tee, got my second onto the green and was left with a twelve-footer. The South African Open now came back into my mind. Once again I was excited and stimulated, but now it helped to have a reference point. I had been in this situation recently and I *knew* what it was like to have one putt for glory. Also, I now remembered a bit of advice about positive thinking that I had been given by John Jacobs: 'If you get nervous over a putt, just remember that you can miss it, or you can hole it; there are no other alternatives.' And if that sounds trite to some, I regard it as good advice. It's the fear of the unknown that causes doubts and creates a confusion in the mind. If you rationalise the situation, the worst thing that can happen is that you miss the putt. So I settled myself down, hit a good putt and I made it.

Now came a different sort of problem altogether – I was in a head-to-head situation, a sudden-death play-off against a man who was one of my heroes. I had been seventeen and a burningly ambitious amateur when Tony Jacklin had won the Open Championship and broken the sequence of overseas domination of *our* greatest tournament. My hero-worship of Tony was no less than that of any other golfing youngster of my generation. I now had to play him – not just the course – for the title. As we sat in the clubhouse, Warren Humphreys, like a good friend, tried to steady me and just before I went out to the first tee he asked, 'Are you going to ask him if he wants to share the first and second place prize-money?' (That is, irrespective of who actually wins.) I wasn't sure; I didn't know whether pros did that because I had never been in this sort of situation before. I had been involved in play-offs before because that was often the way I had been able to pre-qualify for tournaments, creeping in at the last gasp. (In fact I have been in fourteen play-offs during my career and never lost one – which is not, incidentally, the hallmark of a 'choker'!) But I had never been in one involving prize-money. So I answered Warren, doubtfully, 'I don't know.'

Warren then gave me some excellent guidance. 'Tony doesn't need the money,' he said, 'and if you ask him he will probably say "No", and he'll feel one-up so don't mention it.' And I thought: 'Warren's right. Why should Tony want to split with me. The money doesn't really matter to him. He's only interested in the title anyway.' So I said nothing and we stood together on the first tee at Hoylake. On a still day it is one of the most terrifying opening holes anywhere in the world; now, with the wind howling into our faces and darkness falling, I had to play against a man who had won the Open Championship and the US Open in the same year. And the hole was virtually unplayable in the conditions. Still, there were certain things one had to *avoid* doing and the first of these was not to put the tee-shot onto the practice ground. However, I wanted to get as close to the corner of the dogleg as possible because it was still a big second shot; I gambled a little bit, ending up right under the three-foot ridge which runs round the practice area. It meant that I was going to have to hit a fairly lofted shot for my second, which was exactly what I didn't want in that wind.

Tony hit a wonderful tee-shot, right to the corner, and left himself a straight shot, even if it was going to need a one-iron. I gambled again, this time with a four-iron, and it ballooned on me, flirting with out-of-bounds, but in the end left me fifty yards short of the green. I turned my attention to what my opponent was doing. If he got it in the air the wind was going to take it left to right and out of bounds, because that area is only two or three paces from the green. If he went left he would have to chip out of the rough, coming down a hurricane wind on to a hard green with out-of-bounds beyond it. As I saw it, his choice was either something conservative which put him just short of the green or something so flat that the wind could not take it – it was either a one-iron or a driver. It seemed an extraordinary decision to me that Tony finally went for it with a three-wood, but he was the former Open champion, not me. He put the ball on to the second tee, tried to run it through the rough and left himself short of the green. Now he had a tough chip downwind and finally made six the hard way. Meanwhile, I played a flat little chip-and-run to the middle of the green and made five. I had won my first tournament and it was (almost) as pleasant to see two friends, Noel Hunt and Warren Humphreys in third and fourth positions.

Don: Was it really a case of Jacklin losing rather than Mosey winning?

Ian: Well, I'll put it no higher than this. I did a good job to tie him in the last round. I was delighted with four birdies in the last six holes, but most of all I was happy that in my first opportunity to win anything since the South African Open I had done what was required, under pressure.

Don: Your first chance to win anything? You had been runner-up in the French Open earlier in the summer of 1980.

Ian: Ah, but that was an entirely different story. It involved trying to beat Greg Norman over the last eighteen holes and it was never even a remote possibility. As soon as I saw the St Cloud course, I liked it – lovely parkland, the weather dry and the ball running a long way, which was important to me – I'm not a big hitter. And it was a distinguished field. Apart from Norman, it included Johnny Miller and Bob Charles, both Open champions.

Don: And the first-round 66 which saw Ian joint leader with David Ingram prompted one of those starkly realistic pieces from Peter Dobereiner in the *Guardian*:

> Golf is the cruellest game. The player never gets an unplayable delivery from the pavilion end or an unreturnable service or a whack on the ankle as he sets himself for a shot at goal. His failures are his alone. The cruel honesty of the game cannot be ignored in recording that Ian Mosey led the first round of the French Open at St Cloud with 66, six under par. That is no surprise as the Manchester golfer often scores low rounds. He is a good professional and a credit to the game.
>
> Obviously, he could go forward from this point to win but the cruel facts intrude on such speculation. At the age of twenty-eight, in eight years as a professional, his best performance in a major tournament was in the South African Open when, with one putt for victory, he took three

to finish second. Such a record cannot be discounted and, with respectful acknowledgements to Mosey's fine round, harsh reality demands that greater consideration be given to lesser scores by others.

That was absolutely right, the only logical way to look at the position. But the words that leapt out of the page at me were, 'He is a good professional and a credit to the game.' If a writer of Peter Dobereiner's stature thought my son was a credit to his chosen game, I could ask no more. Ian wouldn't share my view of course, but in that moment I wouldn't have cared if he *never* won a tournament so long as one of the game's most respected writers described him as 'a credit to his profession'. That moment, together with the one when my younger boy completed his final year at school as captain of the First XV, having gone through seven years without missing a single game for any reason at any level, have been the best moments of my life.

Ian: I am a notably bad practice-round player and I went out with two mates, John Downey and Gary Logan, and played unbelievably badly. The other two were five years younger than me and I could see them thinking, 'Poor old sod. Why does he bother?' But I had got used to ignoring practice form and went out the following day to shoot my best European tour round up to that point. The second two rounds were tidy; I kept it going and after a second-round 72 I was fourth, behind Maurice Bembridge, Greg Norman and Manuel Ballesteros – distinguished company indeed. A 71 in the third took me to third position, behind Norman and Bembridge. Greg was not yet the force he was soon to become. He was to some extent an unknown quantity, but I knew he had had a lot of success in Australia and the Far East. In fact, I believe at that point he had won one in every three tournaments he had played. He was immensely powerful and he practised all the time. Most of us practised a lot but Greg practised *all* the time. The third of my trio, last out on the final day, was Bernard Gallacher, one of the established British stars.

Norman had a five-shot lead going into that last round and I soon saw something of his power. The first three holes at St Cloud are the biggest on the course and while Bernie and I were hitting medium-irons to the green, Norman was playing eights and nines. The third is a huge par-five, a very well-designed hole with strategically placed bunkers, and it was straight into the wind. To avoid trouble one had to think about a three-wood off the tee, another off the fairway and a nine-iron to the green. Greg hit a driver, then another, and holed the putt for an eagle! His five-stroke lead had become seven and while I had been making fairly solid pars and sort of hanging in there, it was now 'forget it'.

The fifth at St Cloud is a short par-four with about a 60-degree dogleg – very much a positional tee shot, about a three-wood followed by a nice nine-iron to the green. Greg, with a seven-stroke lead, went for the green from the tee and landed his ball on the front edge. He had two more birdies after that and was out in 30. He was just crushing the course with his driver. He hits it so far, and straight, and bold. I remember playing with him in the Greater Manchester at Wilmslow and he went for the first green – twice. Unbelievable.

Anyway, we got to the turn at St Cloud. I had quite a tidy score, one or two under par, but Bernie Gallacher and I were simply watching an exhibition by this time. In fact I had to make a conscious effort to drag my eyes away from Norman's astonishing golf and think about my own. He's such an exciting player that I *wanted* to watch, but I forced myself to get on with my own job and concentrate on my game. I told myself that getting second place in that tournament and in that field was as significant to me as winning, and for someone who had spent so much time in the bottom half of the top 100, that was right. We got to the tenth tee, which is a downhill par-five – for Norman, probably a drive and an eight-iron. He was *interested* in the round at that stage. I don't know what the record winning margin is, but it seemed very much as though Greg had it in mind at that stage, or a record low score – something of that sort. Now, he's a very genial and pleasant man to play with, but just before he actually plays his shot he goes into a cocoon of immense concentration. He takes a long time to get set and nothing must disturb him in that period of preparation. He generates such power off the tee that it requires this high degree of concentration. *Nothing* must disturb it.

Just he was at the top of the backswing on that tenth tee at St

Cloud, his concentration total and absolute, one of the promotion girls, in uniform, stepped out of the crowd and asked him to stop. She had misread a signal from one of the officials down the fairway, thinking the hole was not clear. Greg, however, had sent his caddy down there and had got the all-clear signal, so the interruption which shattered his concentration was twice as galling. He suitably expressed his displeasure, snapped the ball into the trees and made five. After that, from the very set of his body, plainly he had lost interest in records. He just pedalled in – but he still won by ten clear shots!

Don: It's interesting that you make a point about Norman's tremendous concentration, because between shots he's one of those chaps who like to chat. Naturally enough, during on-the-course commentary I never made a remark to a player unless I was replying to one from him. Norman was one of those who frequently like to exchange a friendly word, or to perch on the front of the radio buggy while one of his partners was playing. I remember one occasion at Turnberry, in 1986, when the buggy got stuck in the greasy turf as we tried to cross on the short fourth. Norman was waiting to play – mercifully not yet in the address position – but wanting to get on with it in that unrelenting rain, and when he *had* played, and walked forward to the green, I broke my cardinal rule and spoke first – an apology for delaying his shot. I must say I was surprised by his affability in those circumstances; I can think of one or two Americans who would have been less gracious.

Ian: He is someone I really enjoy playing with. He's a straightforward, approachable and really intelligent player, a no-nonsense character who has the ability to switch on and off. He generates tremendous speed in that swing; it's a very physical thing, not a kind of rippling, flowing sort of movement like Sevvy's. Norman's is a commitment, and the commitment starts when he adopts his address position. You want to watch that address position: it's very careful – he sets his feet, then his grip – it's all done in stages, very much a manufactured preparation which he has made work. And he doesn't ground the driver, either, which is unusual. Everything about his address position is taut, and there is an additional tautness about his concentration. He is one guy you really *know* you mustn't disturb. He winds himself into the shot – a great surge of energy and power from a core of total concentration.

Don: All rather different from Lee Trevino, who was your playing partner during the 1984 Monte Carlo Open. He must have had something to say when you covered the last nine holes at Mont Agel in 29?

Ian: He was pleasant to play with and when I started going well he was tremendously encouraging and helpful. I don't think he enjoyed the course too much himself, however. It was a new tournament, in a very glamorous setting, but because everything on Monte Carlo has to be squeezed into the most convenient small space, the golf course had been sited on top of a mountain. A fortune had been spent on building it because millions of tons of earth had to be moved, and the drive up the Haute Corniche, just to get to the course, was a daunting trip to people like me who are not too keen on heights: half an hour's ascent in a Renault van round a series of hairpin bends – French driver, Gauloise dangling from lips, massively insouciant – with nothing between the van and a sheer drop. And then there's always the return trip to look forward to. Some of us had a little wager, when the event was first announced, on who would be the first to pull out because some of our number are less tolerant than others of – shall we say? – eccentric conditions. Brian Barnes was a clear favourite, and the odds were not too long against my friend Mark James either! In the event, Ian Woosnam got off the plane, drove up to the course, took one look at it and withdrew – only to find that he couldn't get a plane out for another day! Then quite a few more pulled out and this was before we knew about the cloud which settles over the course and plays havoc with tournament organisation.

Don: Now, why should so many want to avoid the course? Was it a touch of vertigo?

Ian: That certainly plays a part. You simply can't play well if you have in your mind that there's a 1,000 foot drop not too far behind you. But also it's a very 'fiddly' course. For example, what is now the eighteenth hole for the tournament – it used to be the ninth – was a par-four which practically anyone in the field could reach with a driver, so they placed a thirty-foot high net along the left-hand side of the tee, making the hole into a ninety-degree dogleg, right to left. As the net stretched for forty feet, a bare patch was very quickly worn in one place on the right-hand side of the tee as everyone tried to play a tee-shot which amounted to a quick hook round the end of the netting. In the second (and what proved to be the last) round I had the wonderful experience of watching one of the great players of all time trying to play a shot which was virtually impossible. Trevino is not renowned as a right-to-left player. He doesn't play *everything* with fade, as some people believe, but let's say his draw is quite subtle. He can hit a nice little chasey hook with an iron and do lots and lots of clever things, but hitting a snap hook off a tee-peg with a driver is not his strong point. His swing goes outside and up; to hit the hook you have to get well inside and spin round on it. So Leroy tried to do the impossible and the ball squirted off at a very strange angle indeed.

Don: Why was it reduced to two rounds?

Ian: Well, it's a long story. When the warm winds from the Sahara hit the massive barrier of rocks which climb up behind Monte Carlo you get a pretty good set of conditions for creating cloud. In the middle of the pro–am the cloud climbed up the rocks and misted everything out. We had been warned what to expect. However, on the first day of the tournament we had lovely, sunny conditions and with birdies at the last two holes I managed a 68, one under par on this trick track. I had done no more than play 'all right'. On the second day I had a late starting time; so had Warren, so we went to inspect the topless beach and went for a swim out to one of the rafts the authorities have thoughtfully anchored seventy or eighty yards out to sea. Looking up at the view, we saw the mountains shrouded in cloud and Warren said, 'I can't believe they are playing up there.' They weren't. When we returned to our hotel to change, Warren rang the tournament office to be told there had been no play since 9 a.m. and we should ring again in an hour. Back we went for another swim, then telephoned again up to Mont Agel. Still no play. Around tea-time, play was abandoned for the day.

The same thing happened the following day, so on Friday and Saturday, Warren and I never even went to the course. There was a bit of confusion then as we set out to try to play thirty-six holes on the Sunday. It was late when Trevino and I

went out and it was pretty clear we were not going to get
thirty-six holes in that day, so we really didn't know whether we
would have to stay over and play on Monday, whether the tournament would be cut simply to thirty-six holes, or what. Anyway,
I started par, par and then had a two at the short third; we
moved on to the two holes which are nearest to the sea – and to
the cliffs! – and the cloud crept up to obscure things once more.
We sat, in a big queue, on the fourth tee for about an hour, and
as soon as there was a break in the cloud I jumped up, played a
hurried tee-shot and dropped two strokes at the par-four fourth.

It was all quite unlike any tournament I had experienced.
There were no leader-boards, and if there had been we would
have had some difficulty in seeing them; the cloud was still
hanging about; we didn't know how many holes were going to
constitute the tournament; and none of us knew where he was
as far as a winning score was concerned. All one could do was
soldier on and hope *someone* knew what was happening.

Then, as I walked to the tenth tee, I met George O'Grady,
the tournament director, and he said that come what may that
round would conclude the tournament – if we could manage to
finish it! So now we knew where we were. I had just birdied the
eighth and ninth and had a couple more at the fourteenth and
fifteenth (the toughest hole on the course), and the putts were
dropping from all sorts of distances. In fact, Willie Aitchison,
caddying for Trevino, described three of them as being from
'illegal' lengths. At last, as we reached the little loop round the
clubhouse, I saw a leader-board. It showed me four strokes
ahead of the field. So from the vaguest possible situation I was
now in a position to win my first European tournament.
Trevino was urging me on and was really supportive. He scored
an eagle two himself at the sixteenth, which got him a bit
interested, but at four strokes behind he was not really in a
position to win unless I did something absolutely stupid. And it
didn't stop him encouraging me, which was something I really
appreciated. A par-three at the seventeenth meant I had now
had eight threes in nine holes and although I missed a distinctly
holeable putt on the last, I had nevertheless come back in 29
and I was a winner in Europe at last.

I am not really a superstitious person but I played the whole of that round with the same ball. In spite of all the delays – I went to the course at 8.20 a.m. and walked off it nine and a half hours later – I didn't *dare* change it!

Don: So Trevino's incessant chatter was not a distracting factor?

Ian: Oh no. He chats all the time and with all the delays there was ample opportunity for him. Some of it is very amusing, some just waffle; it's his way of discharging so much of his energy. In no way at all has it anything to do with putting off his opponent, and I don't think it does distract anyone. After-wards came the champagne reception, with Prince Rainier. I sat with Lee and his wife and it was exceedingly pleasant. During the two following Monte Carlo Opens I attended (as a previous winner) a cocktail party at the palace, on the balcony overlooking the Prince's side of the Marina, and a dinner at the Sporting Club, which has a domed roof which slides open on balmy nights. It was a very glamorous, showbizzy type of week. The players don't regard the tournament with particular affec-tion because the course is not ideal: that ride up to it is hair-raising and we tend not to like razzmatazz during a work-week. But as a bit of a holiday for one's wife it can store up a lot of bonus points.

Don: Your other tournament wins – the Holiday Inns, Smith's Industries and the Kalahari Diamond Classic – have all been in South Africa?

Ian: Yes. Sentimentality does not play a big part in our game but it really is impossible to look back to that Holiday Inns tournament in 1981 without feeling sympathy for Alan Henning. He looked to have the title in the bag when he was penalised two strokes for an irregularity at the ninth hole in his final round. That put him in a three-way play-off with Nigel Burch and myself and at the first extra hole Alan under-clubbed and saw his ball roll into a ditch. Nigel and I both hit the green with my ball slightly further away at ten feet. Henning, in the meantime, had dropped out and got a bad lie. He was already playing four, with the penalty, and when his ball rolled back into the ditch the poor chap conceded. He had had enough for one day. My putt went in, Nigel's stayed out and I was 5,600 rands better off. Some you win, some you don't.

Don: PGA Regulations in 1972 decreed that there was a waiting period of two years before a new professional could make money on the tournament circuit, unless he had achieved full international status as an amateur. In that case, the waiting period was six months, so for someone in Ian's position the obvious time to turn pro was at the end of one summer. By the time the next season came round he would have served his six-month waiting period and be eligible for prize money. The only question was: what to do during the intervening winter months? Unexpectedly, an opportunity arose to take a trip abroad and to play for the first time on a golf course in the United States.

Ian: Peter Wilcock was picked for the World Cup, which meant he had to pull out of a pro–am engagement, with three amateurs, at a resort in Florida. He telephoned me to ask if I could take his place, which was a pleasant surprise, and a bonus, for me. Golf apart, it was an adventure – the first time I had been in a Jumbo jet, and the first time I had seen the American breakfast. What an experience that was for a healthy 21-year-old who liked to start the day with a good meal – a twenty-yard long buffet laden with fresh Florida fruit as well as marvellous crispy bacon, eggs any way you liked them, hash browns, pancakes with maple syrup. And outside, the brilliant sunshine of a perfect day. It was all a far cry from Manchester in December. It was educational, too, to see how brilliantly the Americans organise their leisure.

This was a typical complex with two eighteen-hole golf courses and a miniature course built with great skill as a scaled-down version of the major courses. Thus, while the eighteen-holer we played during the day had the usual quota of man-made water hazards and two holes which ran alongside a river with alligators swimming about in it (all rather exciting),

I went out in the evening to play nine holes of the miniature with one of my amateur partners, a broker from Norfolk, and found that while the biggest hole was about 150 yards long, everything was to scale. It had perfect little bunkers and perfect little water hazards – and *baby* alligators swimming about in the water! Now, that was attention to detail which really impressed me.

I was fascinated, too, by the sight of the Miami Dolphins' coach (before Channel Four had popularised American football in this country) having his own show on one of the local TV stations. The night before the Dolphins played a match the fans could hear from the coach's own lips the details of team changes, fitness reports and the tactics it was intended to adopt in the game. It was like Brian Clough going into Central Television's studios in Nottingham and presenting a programme himself in which he gave Nottingham Forest's fans (and anyone else who was interested) a complete breakdown of how he expected the following day's Football League match to go. Oh, I liked the USA. I could have got very fat if I had stayed to eat their cheesecake and the other sensational puddings they provided for us.

Don: Just a brief glimpse of America, but you have spent more time in Australia and New Zealand. How did you enjoy life there?

Ian: The great bonus about my first visit to Australia (1982) was the chance to see brother Andrew after three years. He had set out on a round-the-world trip in January 1979, which was supposed to last for a year but he has still, in 1989, not yet progressed beyond Sydney. In the early eighties the South African PGA were trying to put together an attractive package of tournaments in the post-Christmas period, with a view to getting more overseas players to take part. This left regulars like myself on their circuit with nothing to do in the period up to Christmas, so it seemed an opportune moment to try Australia for the first time.

I started in Adelaide, led the pre-qualifiers and made every cut so there was no more pre-qualifying after the first one, and I really liked the Australian courses. They are all on or near the coast, so there is always wind and they tend to be big and

demanding as well as tough on the feet. I had tried to quiz some
of the Aussies on the European circuit about the Australian
tour and what most of them said was: 'Wait till you see Royal
Melbourne.' That didn't tell me much about the tour but it did
indicate a degree of unanimity on the popularity of Royal
Melbourne. In due course I saw the course, and although I
didn't make a big cheque there I think it is probably my
favourite course anywhere in the world. It is certainly in my top
three.

Why? Well, to begin with, when you first see it you cannot
appreciate the subtlety of it. In that sense it's a bit like St
Andrews, where it takes a while to understand its real quality.
Now, if you have greens that are very firm (and you can really
only build this sort of course on sand) with seaside grass cut
very tight, you get greens which are lightning fast but will take
spin. You are striking the ball from a similar kind of turf so you
can *impart* spin and there is a measure of control. But in those
conditions the *positioning* of every shot is vital – and it works
from the green back, rather than vice versa as on a watered golf
course. At Royal Melbourne, the greens are so fast and subject
to such subtlety of undulation that you must leave your ball
under the hole at all times. That means that your shot to the
green has to be played from exactly the right position, and so
your tee-shot must go to the right place – you see what I mean
about working backwards from the green? One of them (probably the sixth but I can't remember exactly) is the one hole
which spoils the course. It is just one long slope with no plateau
of any kind and there was trouble one year in the Australian
Open because the green had been cut just *too* fine and when the
wind came up it became impossible. The players were rolling
the ball up the slope and the wind was rolling it back down
again. If the putt was not holed the ball could finish five or six
feet further away from the hole, not just once but time after
time. There was a hold-up on the tee because no one could hole
out and it led to a walk-off. But that is just the one bad hole.

The course otherwise is superb. There is not a single hole on
the course where you can walk onto the tee and just hit the ball.
It has to be positioned, always. Then there has to be control of
the shape of the shot into the green, flight into the green, and

spin. As soon as you water a course or as soon as you have lush fairways you take away one or more of those factors and it becomes a lesser test of pure golfing ability. Royal Melbourne tests every aspect of the game. You cannot tame it by being the biggest hitter or by having a golden touch round the greens. It takes a complete golfer to play it well.

Socially, I enjoyed my time in Australia, especially one or two nights out with small brother. He lives a lifestyle of the eternal student in that he enjoys simple pleasures which can be pursued as cheaply as possible and he gave me probably the best night out I have ever had with a visit to the Comedy Store. That is part of the Jamieson Club in downtown Sydney and we went to an Amateur Night because one of Andrew's friends wanted to try his luck as an entertainer.

The budding Thespian was one Sylvio Offria, born in Egypt of Italian parents, and a resident of Australia since his early teens. He might, upon reflection, have chosen a more suitable venue for his first attempt to pursue his theatrical ambitions because the Comedy Store on Tuesday nights is to Australian culture what a day at the Colosseum was to the citizens of Rome. The audience come not so much to praise Caesar as to bury him. Cries of 'Bravo', 'Encore' and 'Author' are less frequently heard than, 'Girrorf, yer bum.' To make matters worse, Sylvio was an earnest young man who was dreadfully and fatally sincere in his determination to make good on the stage, and he had prepared a routine which brother Andrew, with some experience of Amateur Night (he was as bloodthirsty a Roman as anyone) felt would fall some way short of finding favour with his audience. 'Have you any gags, any one-liners?' he asked Sylvio, who replied that cheap lewdness had no place in his narrative. What exactly had Andrew in mind? Little brother then recounted a story of quite spectacular vulgarity which Sylvio simply failed to comprehend. 'It was at that point,' Andrew warned me, 'that I knew we were in trouble.' Just one further feature was required to produce a recipe for total disaster.

Mr Rodney Rude is one of Australia's foremost entertainers. Over many years on the Australian stage he has refined and perfected a comedy routine which makes Sir Les Patterson sound like Sir John Gielgud playing Lear. He is profoundly and unspeakably blue. But funny with it, as they say. And tonight, recalling his humble origins, he had returned to the Comedy Store as master of ceremonies. Not only would the audience be keyed up as usual to roast anyone foolhardy enough to air his amateur talent on stage but they would have the assistance of Mr Rude to fan the flames – expertly.

The scene was set for the ultimate stage disaster and, feeling a certain loyalty to Andrew's friend the four of us (my wife Mandy and Andrew's girlfriend Diane completed the party) resolved to anaesthetise ourselves as effectively as possible. True to form, my brother had devised a means of doing this. From a local grog shop we smuggled in half a dozen bottles of Jacob's Creek, a pleasant claret-type Australian wine, to supplement the bottle which we were obliged to buy inside the Comedy Store at inflated cost as the price of our table.

Sure enough, Sylvio died the death – but he went down fighting. He was ridiculed mercilessly by Mr Rude and the entire audience but he refused to make a premature departure. He had prepared his script with loving care and he was going to deliver it, come what may. No doubt he already saw himself playing Hamlet: 'This above all, to thine own self be true.' But through all the taunts and insults, through the hail of slings and arrows of outrageous fortune, Sylvio pressed on and completed his routine amidst the most tumultuous crescendo of abuse even Sydney has ever heard. A brave lad. And so it is with delight and admiration that I am able to report a happy ending to this story.

After that début (though I am sure not because of it) Sylvio joined the Sidetrack Theatre Company and then moved on to even better things. In 1988 he was seen on British television screens in the Australian mini-series 'Fields of Fire', playing one of the Italian cane-cutters.

I was not feeling in the pink of condition when I played a practice round with Graham Marsh the following morning. The tournament-proper found me in slightly better health (though not much; Andrew was as glad to see me as I was to see him and we celebrated accordingly) and I managed third place in the New South Wales Open, which paid the expenses of the whole trip for my wife and myself. Andrew caddied for me and enjoyed himself tremendously until the last round, when a lady member of the Manly Club complained that his shorts were too abbreviated and revealing. This startled little brother who replied with some asperity that he had never before encountered such modesty in the local Sheilas. But he had to change.

I must say that the Australian lifestyle has a strong appeal and it was not difficult to see why Andrew's circumnavigation of the globe had faltered in Sydney. My first visit, in 1982, gave me enough OM points to be pre-qualified if I went back the following year; it had been good to see the Rugby-and-tennis-playing member of the family; and the golf in Oz seemed to have a profoundly beneficial influence on my game because I went on to South Africa for two tournaments before Christmas and in that fortnight I shot my lowest nine-hole total (29), my lowest eighteen-hole score (65) and lowest thirty-six-hole (131) and started with two good cheques. So I really needed no persuading to go to Australia for the second time the following winter and to take Mandy with me. Cathay Pacific Airlines provided an excellent deal, with a Hong Kong stopover, splendid in-flight service and a chauffeur-driven limousine to take us to and from the airport in Hong Kong. I had a reasonable tour in Australia apart from the Open, which was played at the Nicklaus-redesigned Australian Club. On the eve of the tournament, Jack announced that he was contributing his appearance money of 50,000 dollars (for flying over from the States to play on the monster he had created) to the prize fund of 175,000 dollars, which made it very big money indeed. And I missed the cut, the only one I have ever missed in Australia, but I didn't feel *too* sorry for myself even though the cut was made at 157. The course is generally regarded as being very nearly unplayable and in hurricane-force winds that year (1983) it *was* unplayable.

Never have I been on a course in such conditions where there were so many shots it was virtually impossible to play – fast-running fairways, lightning greens, American-style huge contours with a wind blowing across them – and sometimes you simply could not stop the ball going into unplayable positions. I remember trying to hit a seven-iron into a par-four hole when I tried to move the ball fifty yards in the air, right to left, to get it into the middle of the green. No other shot would do; if it went one inch too far, the ball went all the way because wind and slope were in the same direction. So I shot 159 and retired without overwhelming regret.

Tweed Heads, on the NSW-Queensland border, was an interesting experience because the club's wealth is based on batteries of poker machines and it was fascinating to find a golf clubhouse housing two whole floors of gaming machines. Eamonn Darcy's girlfriend was a friend of Mandy's and she asked if she could accompany us to Coolangatta, where the Tweed Heads course is situated. I rented the most expensive apartment I have ever occupied, overlooking that very blue Pacific and with the deepest snow-white carpet throughout. It cost far more money than I wanted to pay, but the girls fell in love with it at first sight so we were stuck there for the week. I remember coming back one afternoon after an early start and lying in this deep carpet with these two lovely ladies providing me with beer in one hand and avocado dip in the other with Australia *v*. England Test cricket on one TV channel and the tournament in which I was playing on the other, the remote control at my side. The thought flickered across my mind that if I were to die at that moment it wouldn't be too bad a way to go.

During that tournament Jack Newton was living in the same apartment block, and while I had known him on the European tour he was in a league above me and I had had very little to do with him in any personal way. At Coolangatta I got to know him very well – a delightful man as well as a superb golfer – and so I was desperate sorry when his accident occurred shortly after that. (He lost an arm and an eye and suffered other horrifying injuries from the propeller of a light aircraft.)

Don: I knew him perhaps better than you at that stage after reporting quite a lot of his golf in Britain, and particularly a win in the Benson and Hedges International at Fulford, where he started with three birdies and an eagle in the final round after a rather colourful night out. Three years after his accident I was in New Zealand and was asked to go into the Radio NZ studios in Christchurch to take part in a morning music-and-chat programme, Jimmy Young style. When I arrived the producer asked me to wait a minute or two because another interviewee was already in the studio. I listened to the voice for half a minute and then said, 'That's Jack Newton, isn't it?' The producer replied, 'Yes. Do you know him?' 'Put me in with him, please,' I pleaded and after a quick word on the talk-back with the programme presenter he ushered me into the studio. Jack Newton and I were supposed to do five to ten minutes of chat each with music in between the conversation. As I remember it we spent the rest of the morning in the studio with the presenter simply changing the drift of the conversation slightly from time to time. We talked about the 1975 Open at Carnoustie (which Jack was so disappointed not to win), the Benson and Hedges, about mutual friends like Neil Hawke and Arthur Clues (a great Australian Rugby League player who was also a good cricketer), about Jack's accident and his new life in PR and promotion. His injuries were indeed horrifying if one dwelt on them, but such was that remarkable man's zest for life, his enthusiasm for his new career, his humility about his past achievements and his total absence of any trace of self-pity that the time simply streaked by. If I had produced that programme, or presented it, I would have felt very proud. Jack Newton created a magic piece of broadcasting; he is a very similar type to our mutual friend, Neil Hawke.

Ian went on to New Zealand from that second visit to Australia, largely because I rather pushed him into it. I had formed a great attachment to the country, and its people, some years earlier and I took – still take – every opportunity to return. So I hoped my son and daughter-in-law would enjoy a visit for two tournaments.

Ian: No one on earth, I suppose, could enjoy New Zealand quite as much as my father. It's a bit quiet for my taste; in fact my abiding memory of Christchurch is that it is the quietest place I have ever seen in my life – unbelievably quiet. I played in Christchurch with Wayne Riley, then a brash, green kid, and he gave me the usual Australian story: 'You know, when the plane lands in Christchurch the pilot tells passengers, "Adjust your watches please. Put them back thirty-five years."'

Don: Yes, but did any New Zealanders offer you their views on the Australians? No? Well, that would be because they are worlds apart in terms of courtesy but, believe me, they have some pungent and colourful views on their Pacific neighbours. Anyway, you got on well enough with the New Zealanders.

Ian: We met impossibly kind hospitality in both Christchurch and Auckland, where I really loved the Titirangi course – lovely turf, tight, treelined fairways, delightful with its displays of rhododendrons. It was a good trip.

Don: There seems to be an increasing interest amongst European pros in the Australian circuit these days.

Ian: That's right, but the dates of the tour in Australia make it difficult to go there and do the full Sunshine tour. I must mention my regret at the loss of Zimbabwe (or Rhodesia when I knew it) from the Sunshine circuit. When we played the Victoria Falls Classic at Elephant Hills the country was virtually at war with the two different factions of guerillas, Nkomo's and Mugabe's, fighting against Ian Smith's administration, and a mile-wide minefield stretched around the town. If you hit your golf ball very far into the rough you were quite likely to stumble over an anti-terrorist patrol crouching in the bush. The Viscount aircraft flying into the airport had to make their approach in a strange, and dicey, spiralling descent to avoid the heat-seeking missiles which the guerrillas could launch from the jungle. (It was one of these which, misguidedly targeted on the kitchens of the Elephant Hills clubhouse, ultimately destroyed it.)

That was the grim side of playing there. On the other hand there was the lovely old Colonial-style hotel, barely 500 yards from the breath-taking Victoria Falls, where we were accommodated. I was a great jogger in those days and it was wonderful to start the day by trotting along the path which fringes the Falls and watching the rainbow form as the early morning sunlight caught the spray.

Don: It certainly is one of the great naturally beautiful spectacles of the world; I brought back some photographs of the Falls from a Rugby tour in 1961, but at that time you were rather more interested in the Zulu shield and spear in my collection of souvenirs!

Ian: One of the great delights of Rhodesia was the company

of one of golf's most colourful characters, Simon Hobday, who
is the subject of more legend and folklore than anyone else in the
game. In fact he went white when I mentioned that we were
writing this book, but I assured him that due discretion would
be observed. The first time I saw him in his role as a course
jester was playing the eighteenth at Portmarnock in the Irish
Open. He was with Des Smyth who, of course, had a
tremendous following as they approached the last green. At this
point, Hobday took out of his golf bag a Viking helmet, horns
and all, and put it on as he played a very difficult pitch over the
corner of a bunker – and holed the shot. How the crowd loved it
– until Des thought he had better join in, borrowed the helmet,
and three-putted!

With his luxuriant growth of hair and wild, piratical
moustache, Hobbers *was* a Viking. A great entertainer, but
also a magnificent golfer. In talking about Freddie Trueman's
cricketing days you have always insisted that to be a great
sporting personality it is necessary first to be a great performer,
and that is absolutely true of Simon Hobday. He's a good
friend, a warm and generous host. Before he left Rhodesia,
shortly after independence and it became Zimbabwe, he used
to entertain hordes of players as guests in his home in Salisbury
(now Harare) and one year the company included Mandy and
myself, Warren Humphreys and his wife, Andrew Chandler
and his wife, Bill Longmuir and Gary Baleson (a South African
player). As Simon and his wife have three children it all
promised to be a bit crowded, but no one worried about that.
Oh yes, and there was the dog. A schizophrenic dog. He comes
into the story, too.

Hobbers had had a big lead in the Elephant Hills tournament and let the prize slip away from him, so when the rest of
the party arrived at his home (he caught an earlier plane) he
had been drowning his sorrows for some time. We had a
splendid party and the following day there was a thirty-six-hole
pro–am at Wingate. Simon shot 66, 64 to win by ten strokes and
celebrated by joining his guests in an all-night session. There
were then two days to recover before the Rhodesian Open.
Simon shot 68, 69, but was still a few strokes behind Dennis
Watson. On the night before the third round he climbed into his

dinner jacket and black tie and went off to the dinner at which the Rhodesian Sportsman of the Year was announced. At 4 a.m. he returned home, legless – absolutely legless – and woke everybody up. He'd won the title. He was absolutely delighted at being voted his country's outstanding sportsman of the year, so his guests were invited (or instructed, depending upon how you look at it) to join him in drinking champagne out of the trophy as dawn began to break. Hobday didn't go to bed at all and shot 65 when he returned to the little matter of the Rhodesian Open. A last-round 68 gave him a tie for the lead and he then won the play-off. So in a week he had won a pro–am by ten clear strokes, been elected Rhodesia's Sportsman of the Year and won his country's Open Championship. It had been a memorable week for all of us, with just one possibly discordant note in the form of a terrifying experience for Bill Longmuir.

It is now time to introduce the Hobday dog – the dog with the split personality. It was a bull terrier and, quite unlike most of its breed, was gentle, lazy and indolent, spending most of its days supine and raising its head occasionally to accept a pat, a stroke, a fondling of the ears. It was utterly unlike any other bull terrier of my acquaintance anywhere in the world – until a key word was uttered by its master. We shall not dwell upon the word in case it should chance to be one which triggers a reaction in *all* creatures of the species. Suffice it to say that it is not a word which is likely to figure prominently in the debates of Brent Council. When the word was uttered the limp bundle of canine docility was instantly transformed into a snarling, slavering, slobbering monster. It was as if it had been subjected to a double shot of rabies virus and in that moment it was entirely capable of taking on, single-pawed, a charging herd of rogue elephants.

The genial Longmuir, returning from a pleasantly convivial evening in Salisbury, now decided that it would impolite to switch on the lights as he returned to the Hobday household and began to pick his way carefully through the darkness and the slumbering multitudes who were accommodated on settees, in cupboards, on the floor. *And he stepped on the dog.* It had to be the worst moment of his life. He remembered nothing of the affectionate family pet which, for the past week, had been only too happy to welcome him to the Hobday home. He remembered only the drooling Baskerville menace into which it could be so rapidly transformed. His blood turned to ice and he stood motionless in the darkness awaiting his fate. All too clearly he realised that he was standing directly above the dog; he remembered with awful clarity having heard a story about how mediaeval bull-baiting was carried out and how the bull terrier, once its teeth had closed over the most vulnerable (and most prized) part of the bull's anatomy, could never be prised loose. But the dog muttered drowsily, licked his ankle, rolled over and went back to sleep.

Now let's have a flashback in the career of Simon Hobday because, quite frankly, I am fascinated by Hobbers. This is not simply because he is a good friend, or because he is such a colourful character, or even because he is a tremendously good golfer. It is a combination of all these factors, plus his passionate patriotism as a Rhodesian and his determination to bring honour to what was his country until it became Zimbabwe and, with infinite sadness, he moved out.

Simon tried for years to get into the Open Championship, which is, of course, not easy at the best of times with all the pre-qualifying requirements. His attempts met with every sort of disaster, (despite the fact that he was always a good enough golfer to be in that company) from three-putting the final green on a qualifying course and missing out by one stroke to turning up at the wrong course at the wrong time. The number of ways in which things went wrong had become a legend on the circuit, and after seven years of failure it had become something of an obsession with him. While the rest of us waited and wondered what sort of exotic disaster could overtake Hobbers in each succeeding year, he was finally heading for success at last in 1975, playing at St Andrews to prequalify for that year's Open at Carnoustie. At last, everything was going right; he was steaming away towards a score which would put him in with shots to spare when he reached the Road Hole. All he had to do was avoid the trap and he would be in the Open at last. And he knocked it into the sand! Now, it's Clive Clark's story, really, because he was Simon's playing partner and I've heard him describe it as rather like the TV advertisement for Hamlet cigars, only there was to be no happy ending to this story. The bunker is so deep that unless you are standing right on the lip you can't see what is happening down in the sand and Clive *heard* Simon have a couple of goes at it but no ball appeared on the green. Then Hobbers gave it a big thrash and fired the ball over the green onto the road, and he was looking at an eight or nine – and another missed Open. Now, when a player has had a disaster like that you like to give him a lot of space. Muttered words of sympathy are no good to anyone. You keep out of the way, avoid the gaze. So Clive now stood and awaited the emergence of the disconsolate figure from the bunker. But no one appeared.

After a few minutes Clive thought the time had come to investigate, so he walked across and stood looking down into the abyss. There was his partner's figure, prostrate in the sand, arms and legs outstretched, eyes closed. It required no great imagination to guess what was going through his mind. Seven years of toil to make it into the Open, and now it had got away from him again. Of all the golf holes in the world, the seventeenth at St Andrews must have caused more anguish, more despair, more fleeting thoughts of suicide, than any other. Clive just about qualified as a psychiatric nurse in persuading Hobbers to climb out of the sand and complete the round – with his heart in his shoes and his mind in a turmoil. But his agonies were still not at an end.

In 1976, Simon won the German Open and earned exemption from pre-qualifying for Royal Birkdale. At last, incredibly, he had made it. He was now utterly determined to make up for all those years of disappointment by having a good Open, and he played no fewer than nine practice rounds, preparing himself to the nth degree for the world's greatest golf tournament. As he strode to the first tee, with hope in his heart and confidence in his mind that he could have done no more to equip himself for his contest with the course, he put his foot in a sprinkler-hole, twisted his ankle and had to withdraw from the Open!

11   *Radio Links*

Don: Golf commentary on radio is a relatively recent development. For many years radio's coverage was a two-man operation with John Fenton as the producer and Tom Scott, at that time editor of *Golf Illustrated*, as reporter, commentator, interviewer and anything else that was required. A commentary position of modest dimensions was placed somewhere overlooking the eighteenth green at most tournaments, certainly at the Open, and from there Tom, with relaxed expertise and that lovely Scots accent which always seems just right for describing golf, did almost all his broadcasting. He knew all the top professionals (and amateurs) well and they all knew him. Descriptions of play on the final green were carried out with an attention to detail but without hyperbole; interviews were conducted on a basis of mutual respect. Only once was he, almost, thrown out of his stride. That was in 1971 when the 22-year-old Bernard Gallacher had come in early on the last day of the Martini International with a score which seemed likely to hold up as the rest of the field followed him home and Bernard was beguiled into starting a fairly early celebration of victory. The score *did* hold up and when the time came to interview him Tom's first question naturally enough referred to the fact that it had been a long wait for the young man. What had he done to while away the time? 'Och, Mr Scott,' said Bernard, 'I've just been sitting here getting quietly pissed.'

In the mid-sixties, George Bayley, a county golfer in Northumberland *and* Durham who was also a freelance broadcaster, submitted a blueprint for extending golf commentary from the fringes of the eighteenth green and taking it out on to the course. The idea was not taken up at the time because of the expense involved but it was not forgotten by John Fenton, as BBC Radio's executive golf producer, and when more money became available for outside broadcasts in the 1970s he was

quick to put the suggestion forward once again. On-the-course
commentary was introduced and became a regular feature of
Saturday and Sunday afternoon sports programmes in particular, and during major tournaments like the Open, and one or
two others, it was employed in mid-week Sports Desks (Radio
2) as well. From the first it was recognised that radio could
never compete with television in its coverage of golf.

From modest beginnings, due to having too few cameras to
cover much of the play until it neared the clubhouse, television
golf has become brilliant broadcasting. The BBC have been
fortunate in having a succession of producers who were not
simply technically accomplished; in addition, they have had
a real feeling for the game. And BBC TV were blessed in
arriving fairly quickly at an ideal pairing of commentators
in Henry Longhurst and Peter Alliss – probably the most
accomplished and entertaining duo we have known in any form
of sports commentary.

In radio we set out first and foremost to provide an *information*
service to listeners who could not be at the tournament and who
had no access to a television set. But within that broad
framework there was no reason why we should not strive to
make the actual broadcasting, the provision of the information,
as interesting and colourful as possible. So reporters were sent
out, on foot, with an engineering colleague carrying twenty
pounds of equipment on his back, to describe individual rounds
(and pairings) as they happened. It was not easy (especially for
the burdened engineer) on a hot summer's day – because we *did*
have sunny 'Opens' at one time – to fight one's way through the
crowds on the last two days of the world's greatest tournament,
to get into a position where shots could be observed without
obtruding into the player's direct or peripheral vision, and to
describe them *sotto voce* yet audibly to the listener. But it was
fun. And from a purely subjective point of view, it was exciting
broadcasting. From 1980 (Muirfield) onwards, we were
allowed to operate from electrically driven buggies, which came
as a great relief to the engineering side of our team and a
welcome alternative to reporters with bad feet, like me.

My involvement in golf broadcasting began in the mid-
sixties and it came about because when the Open was staged at

Royal Lytham or Royal Birkdale it was on 'my' manor, so to speak, as the senior outside broadcasts producer in the north of England. Similarly, when other tournaments were played at, say, Gosforth Park, Lindrick, Fulford, Royal Liverpool, Ganton, Hillside and other great courses in the Region, it was my job to arrange the setting up of the broadcasting facilities there. John Fenton had long been my closest friend in the Outside Broadcasts Department and we developed a very happy working relationship.

Commentary of all sorts – cricket, Rugby, state and ceremonial occasions – was still a spare-time occupation for me but as it developed I became increasingly attracted to the idea of on-the-course descriptions of golf. First, though, there was at least one hair-raising production experience to survive. On the never-to-be-forgotten occasion in 1969 when Tony Jacklin started the upward trend of British professional golf, Tom Scott had described his Open Championship victory at Royal Lytham in a marvellously emotional piece of commentary. Two hours later, as John Fenton and I started to put together all the bits and pieces of tape which described a historic day we made the horrifying discovery that the actual moment of Jacklin's win, as well as his triumphant walk up the eighteenth fairway to the cheers of an ecstatic crowd, had been 'wiped' by an over-zealous engineering colleague. There was no record on tape of what was, arguably, the greatest moment in British golf up to that point. It is a brilliant piece of improvisation by Messrs Fenton and Scott which now lies in the BBC archives, a recording of the finish of the 1969 Open manufactured from retrospective commentary by Tom Scott (looking at a scene far removed from that he describes on tape) and accompanied by sound effects from the recorded programme library.

Royal Lytham was the scene of broadcasting embarrassment of a different kind during the 1977 Ryder Cup match. I was at the tail-end of the field, reporting Nick Faldo's notable win over Tom Watson; up ahead of me was a colleague, John Helm, covering the Nicklaus–Gallacher match, and he decided to call for a comment from one of the celebrities following that particular singles. 'Among the many showbiz personalities who are keen golfers,' Helm told listeners blithely, 'is Bruce Forsyth.

How d'you think this is going, Bruce?' There was a brief, but perceptible pause before the hissed reply: 'It's true I am keen on golf. It is also true that I know something about the etiquette of the game. Don't stick that thing [microphone] under my nose when Jack Nicklaus is putting.'

Now, not much live broadcasting goes on in radio today. Indeed, sports outside broadcasts represent one of the last bastions. So perhaps showbiz people may be forgiven for believing that *everything* is recorded as 99 per cent of *their* artistry is recorded. Bruce had fallen into that trap, and when the players had holed out he hurried after John Helm to say, 'Now then, young man. You didn't mind me putting you straight back there, did you? You can take it out of the recording, can't you? What is it you want to know?' To my eternal regret I learned later that Helm did not tell Brucie that he had gone out 'live', not only to Radio 2 listeners but to the countless millions tuned in to World Service as well.

And it was Royal Lytham again, this time during the 1979 Open, which provided one of my most enjoyable moments of golf commentary. That was when Severiano Ballesteros *destroyed* his playing partner, Hale Irwin, with a staggering exhibition of golf. Irwin was playing immaculate, typically American stuff – bang-bang-putt (for either a birdie or, at worst, a par) for hole after hole. Sevvy was spraying his tee-shots everywhere, but the recovery would come sailing over obstructions of every kind to plop on to the green, and as often as not the putt would drop into the hole. On the short fifth my engineering colleague and I had great difficulty in getting into position to describe the putts and we certainly didn't get there as quickly as our producer, sitting snugly in his caravan behind the stands around the eighteenth green, wanted. Never having been out on a golf course in his life, much less broadcast from one on the final day of the Open, he had no conception of the difficulties involved. Fighting my way through the crowd carrying micro-phone, clipboard and stopwatch (always needed since many reports require precise timing of durations like one minute, one minute thirty or forty seconds, and so on) presented problems enough; for my colleague, humping his twenty-pound pack with a tall aerial, they were very much more acute. The producer simply did not understand the situation, so I decided to make it crystal clear in my next piece. I then announced to the world that crowd-control was getting out of hand and prophesised an absolute shambles if something was not done about it – and quickly.

We got through the long sixth and as we faced the wide expanse of the seventh hole, alongside the railway line with crowds only on the left of the fairway, a stalwart figure loomed in front of me. 'Now then, you moaning bastard – is this clear enough for you?' Mel Whittle, chief of stewards but better known to me as secretary of Fylde Rugby Union Club, was in that context a good friend of mine. 'Fine,' I replied tersely. 'Keep it like that and we'll have nothing to complain about.' We completed the seventh, eighth and ninth without mishap. On the tenth, Sevvy was in the elephant grass on the left, as usual, and it was becoming a bit repetitive to describe recoveries from such positions so I moved off, way out to the right of Hale Irwin who had rather a tight lie. This was the last year in which the Open started on Wednesday and finished on Saturday, by the way. Keep that in mind.

As Irwin addressed the ball he was suddenly conscious of a figure directly behind him, a figure who should certainly not have been standing twenty yards to a player's rear in the final round of the 1979 Open Championship – an elderly lady holding two shopping baskets! Almost plaintively he addressed himself to a police chief inspector accompanying the match: 'What is *she* doing there? Who is she?' As if coping with the wayward genius of Ballesteros was not enough . . .

Chief Inspector to lady with shopping: 'Now then, love, I'm afraid you are putting the player off by standing there. How do you come to be here, anyway?'

Lady shopper: 'I always come across this way with my shopping on a Saturday. Why, is there something special on today?'

With great glee I reported incident and dialogue to Radio 2 listeners. We completed the tenth and eleventh. At the short twelfth, out of the shrubbery sprang the chief of stewards. He was not pleased with me.

I suppose that is as near as I have come to physical injury during an Open Championship, but the 1977 occasion at

Turnberry ran it close on two counts. On the second day, while I was following the colourful Trevino, someone in London (from whom all blessings flow) decided it would be a good idea to 'mix' Radio 2 and Radio 3 at the tea interval in the Test Match at Old Trafford and to have the Alderman (normally heard on 'Test Match Special') from the Open Golf Championship talking to Brian Johnston, who was in the commentary box in Manchester. No one stopped to think that Turnberry is one of the problem courses as far as radio transmission is concerned because in one or two areas of the Ailsa course it is not possible to get a clear signal. It was close to one of these areas that I now stood – the seventh fairway. If I went to the side of the fairway and stood in the rough I would be completely inaudible; if I remained in my present position, which was where, approximately, tee-shots on the seventh usually landed, I *could* be heard.

'Stay just where you are,' came the instructions from the producer – as usual, with absolutely no idea of what was involved. So while Jack Nicklaus and two others stood on the seventh tee waiting to play, two idiots festooned with broadcasting equipment stood in the middle of the fairway in front of them.

'Hello, Alderman,' crooned Brian Johnston from Old Trafford, 'how nice to be talking to you in the Open Championship. Where exactly are you?'

'In the middle of the seventh fairway, BJ,' I replied, 'and three of the world's top golfers are 250 yards behind me and trying to drive.'

'Oh, I'm sure they won't mind waiting a minute while you bring us up to date with what's happening there,' replied Brian.

He was, of course, entirely wrong. As the dialogue continued, jocularly from Brian's end, nervously from mine, a golf ball whistled over my head. The great Nicklaus, tiring of waiting for two lunatics to remove themselves from his path – and very rightly so – had fired his warning-shot not so much across the bows as over the top-mast. My colleague and I reacted promptly and 'Test Match Special' was left to complete the filling of the tea interval at Old Trafford from its own resources.

The final round at Turnberry led to one of the great climaxes of The Open, between Nicklaus and Tom Watson, but from a commentary point of view it was – dare one say it? – almost boring. For sixteen holes the two Americans matched each other, Watson driving impeccably to the middle of the fairway, Nicklaus usually finding the light rough, but both hitting their approach shots to the middle of the green. It then became a matter of a winning putt dropping and it didn't happen until the long seventh, where Watson scored a birdie and Nicklaus had to be content with a par. One hole to play, Watson a stroke in front. Nicklaus, going for the big one, blocked his tee-shot out to the right and the ball came to rest in difficult circumstances which involved a clump of gorse; Watson, playing safe, had taken an iron from the tee and was lying in a prime position on the fairway about a seven-iron shot from the green. The crowd surged over to the right and as Nicklaus played a wondrous shot to the green – and sank the putt – the situation was described by (a) nearest to Nicklaus, an American commentator, (b) me and (c) on my left, a Japanese broadcaster. As the shot winged its way towards the green I uttered a few trite words and was then crunched flat into the turf by the crowd who raced for a position to see the final putts of the 1977 Open Championships. I remember croaking feebly, 'Over to Desmond Lynam behind the eighteenth green' as I was trampled into the dust, along with my American and Japanese colleagues. The rest is history: Nicklaus sank that marvellous long putt but Watson, having played to six feet, sank his as well. I never saw any of that but the spike-marks from a hundred spectators' shoes were imprinted in my back for months afterwards.

In those days the on-the-course commentators were accompanied on the final day by an expert comments man, in my case Dai Rees, with whom I had a wonderful relationship which I shall always treasure. The other seasoned professional doing this job was Eric Brown, doughty fighter of Ryder Cup matches and magnificently Glaswegian in expressing his views. At that time he was landlord of a pub in Edinburgh. Before the start of the 1980 Open at Muirfield my fellow on-the-course commentator, Chris Rea (the Scottish and British Lions centre-three-quarter and, as a graduate of St Andrews University, very much a golf man, too), went sick.

For the first three days I did the course commentary on my

own and on the final day John Fenton (having by this time
given up the production to the newly arrived Gordon Turnbull
to take over keeping all the scores up to date from the Press
Centre) was due to go out with Eric Brown. Now Fenters is one
of the nicest people God ever made, but he was a trifle nervous
on this occasion about doing something with which he was not
familiar. He is master of his own trade; he was uncertain about
how he might be at another. But the job had to be done. I would
go out for the final round with Watson and Ken Brown while
John accompanied the pair immediately preceding them.

Eric Brown's fondness for a dram or two was well known within the game and thus, when he put his head through the door of
our radio caravan on the Sunday morning and announced that
he was going to the PGA tent for 'a wee chat' I thought it might
be advisable to keep him closer to home in the couple of hours
before we all went out with the leaders. We had a certain amount
of 'hospitality' available there so Eric settled down companion-
ably over a glass or two of Scotch. It all began innocently enough.

'Don, you've never been to see me in my pub.'

'No, Eric. To begin with I don't know where it is.'

'Och, there's nay bother. Ye pass it every time you go to
watch Hairts.'

'But I don't go to watch Heart of Midlothian, Eric. In fact
I don't go to watch football at all and certainly not in
Edinburgh.'

'Ay, I ken that noo. But ye go to watch Rugby at Murrayfield
and ye have to pass my door to get there. Ye must call tae see us
– the only pub in Scotland wi' live music seven nights a week.'

That seemed as good a reason as any for *passing* the portals of
the Brown hostelry but while I was trying to think of a suitable
response, J. Fenton popped his head into the caravan and
blanched with horror at the sight of his on-the-course colleague
of the afternoon happily contemplating what was probably his
sixth double Scotch. He beckoned me out.

'You irresponsible fool, ' he hissed, in the way that one old
friend can abuse another, 'how could you let him get stoned
before we even go out onto the course?'

Lamely, I put the point that it was better to have the bibulous
Mr Brown under our personal supervision than roaming freely

with his mates in the PGA marquee. My friend was not convinced that this had been the wisest course to adopt and finally went out for duty with his expert comments man in the manner of a French aristocrat approaching the guillotine in his tumbril. His worst fears, I regret to say, were realised.

Somewhere out on the fairways the pair of them encountered Clive Clark, doing *his* on-the-course work for television. At some stage of his playing career, Clive had been the subject of a newspaper misprint – a 'literal', as it is known in the trade – and his name had appeared as 'Olive'. This appeared to have stuck in the minds of some of his fellow professionals. Mr Brown, now positively oozing bonhomie, hailed him: 'Hey, Olive. How are ye?' Clive, recognising the signs only too well, chose to ignore the greeting and departed as quickly as he could. He was followed by an anguished cry from the former Ryder Cup captain, 'Olive, you miserable ——. D'ye think ye're too good to talk to me because ye're working for —— television.' My friend Fenton shrank as low as he could into the long grass as this colourful exchange was picked up by the multitudes thronging the course at that point. To this day he blames me for Eric's lively state. I insist that it could have been a lot worse if he had gone to the PGA stand.

Meanwhile I was suffering a little myself. We had, 'presenting' the programme from the commentary position behind the eighteenth green, a young man who shall remain nameless because he has since gone on to better things and it would be wrong to blight his professional life. But he was not good at that time. His knowledge of his own language was a trifle imperfect and when he ventured into the realms of simile he was liable to out-do anything Mrs Malaprop might have dreamed up. Thus, when the tall American, Andy Bean, marched up the eighteenth fairway, our friend behind the green announced to the world: 'And here comes Andy Bean, striding onto this eighteenth green – like Goliath into the Colosseum.' At the end of the Watson–Brown round (and how bravely Ken played in the company of the brilliant Watson), some three hours later, I accosted our producer: 'If that moron [X, in the commentary box] is involved in the Open next year, count me out.' X *was* involved in 1981 at Sandwich; I counted myself out.

The young Ballesteros first really came to international notice in the 1976 when he was locked in a head-to-head tussle with Johnny Miller on the last day at Royal Birkdale, and I was producing the 'Sport on Two' coverage from Southport while Chris Rea was reporting this battle royal out on the course. Chris, John Helm and I were sharing a 'family room' in a local boarding-house for the duration of the tournament and after just one night, Chris was complaining bitterly (with some support from John) about my snoring. He even went to the lengths of taking a Uher recording machine into the room and entertaining our colleagues the following day by playing back the fruits of his nocturnal labours. I tartly pointed out that I couldn't help a natural function like snoring and it was a pity he had nothing better to do at night than mess about with a futile recording. Chris decided on a more drastic course of action.

During the next evening's tour of local hostelries he 'acquired', in best Rugby style, a handbell from one of the pubs we visited and resolved (in concert with the delighted Helm) to wait until my snoring reached its highpoint and then ring the bell furiously in my ear. He made just one mistake. Chris is not as good with a pint as I am and so he fell asleep before I did, still with the bell secreted under his bedclothes. He did, in fact, achieve his objective of waking me in the middle of the night, not through the agency of handbell-ringing but with a demented scream of agony. He had rolled over in his sleep, bringing the most delicate part of his anatomy into sudden and painful contact with the bell. He was not too happy, either, when during the following day's broadcasting, I made a producer's inquiry about why he was speaking in a much higher-pitched voice than usual.

But Chris, over the years, has become used to vicissitudes of all kinds, like the occasion when he and his engineering colleague drove into a ditch at Sunningdale from which they could not extricate the buggy, and it was from a distinctly undignified position, surrounded by a highly amused crowd – not yet ready to be helpful – that he carried out one of his more memorable two-minute reports.

Chris was, in fact, one of the pioneers of on-the-course golf commentary and he had a foretaste of some of the adventures to come when he was following Jack Newton, partnered by Bobby Cole from South Africa, in the 1975 Open at Carnoustie. For reasons which did not seem relevant at the time the producer decided he would like an interview with Newton's beautiful blonde wife while she watched her husband play. The engineer with Chris was Ken Keen, who was a pioneer of this form of broadcasting, spending very long hours indeed trying to perfect the quality of the signal which came back to the control point from various parts of the course. Ken, with the equipment on his back, was holding the microphone between Chris and the fair Mrs Newton as they talked when a tractor, driven by a member of the greenkeeping staff and towing a small, low trailer, approached from Ken's rear. The trio had picked their spot for the interview away from the crowds thronging the fairways and thus were not prepared for traffic. What was more, Ken Keen, absorbed in balancing the levels of the two voices, was far too busy even to *hear* the approach of the tractor.

What happened next might as well have taken hours to film in a Hollywood comedy sequence to get it just right, and most certainly it could never have been achieved in one 'take'. But truth has ever been stranger than fiction. The tractor now passed behind Ken and the trailer, swinging slightly in its wake, nudged him in that particularly sensitive area behind the knees. Taken completely off guard and still concentrating utterly on the broadcasting, Ken toppled backwards – and landed in the trailer! The tractor-driver failed to hear any startled cry or notice any increase in his load and continued on his way towing a trailer and a senior BBC engineer. It left Chris and Mrs Jacqui Newton gazing at each other in a state of near-hysteria. Meanwhile, back at the presenter's position behind the eighteenth, Desmond Lynam found the interview cut off in mid-flow for reasons unknown and had to limp out of the silence with, 'We seem to have lost Chris Rea and Jacqui Newton . . .' Poor Ken Keen, who had indeed been lost, never got a mention.

Golf gave me so many *good* memories to savour in my twilight broadcasting years. It was always an enormous privilege, I felt, to be out with the men who were heading towards an Open Championship win and since everyone has a favourite, let me say that mine was ever Tom Watson. I used to hold the view that he was actually put together by a computer. His swing always seemed, to my untutored eye, to be perfect; certainly his good manners and his sense of PR were absolutely perfect, and this is perhaps best illustrated by an occasion when he won at Royal Birkdale. As he hovered over an eagle putt a small child in the crowd round the green let out a cry. Watson stepped back from the putt but never glanced in the direction of the distraction. He weighed up the situation again, missed the putt (but at least got a birdie) and then paused in his walk to the next tee. 'Now, where's my young supporter?' he asked with that engaging, All-American boy smile.

In spite of all this, my heart bled for Nick Price at Troon in 1983 when just one stray tee-shot almost certainly cost him the Open title won by Watson. For once I had deserted Watson, who was up ahead, to stay with the young South African when he drove into light rough at the thirteenth. He had been making a tremendous charge up to that point and it seemed that nothing could stop him. But by straying fractionally off-line from the tee he was not able to reach the green with his second. He dropped a shot and never recovered his momentum. I have since seen this described as 'blowing' his chance, but that is a cruel verdict. Pressure certainly affected Simon Owen when he was in contention at St Andrews in 1978 and is it, I wonder, even remotely fair to criticise a man in that position when he was competing, head to head, with Jack Nicklaus for the Open Championship? Golf can indeed be a cruel game.

It was during that 1978 Championship that we tried an experiment of siting a fixed commentary position behind the seventh and eleventh greens with the intention of covering holes seven, eight, nine, ten and eleven on the final day. Dai Rees and I stood there with a marvellous view of the St Andrews loop, but in the last round, with all the contenders involved at once, it was a near-impossible task to keep an eye on what was happening simultaneously on five holes. Without the superb Dai it could not even have been attempted.

On the first three days I operated alone – there was no great problem at that time – and I was driven out to the loop each morning in a BBC Scotland truck. On the Friday, returning from this errand, the driver was horrified to see a front wheel fall off and roll straight into the champagne tent. It is good to report that no glasses were broken, no bubbly spilled. But Christie O'Connor (Himself) *was* disturbed at breakfast!

'Opens' were not the only assignments on the golf circuit. I have had the great pleasure of describing play in the Benson and Hedges Internationals at Fulford, the Dunlop Masters at a variety of venues, the European Open at Royal Liverpool and Sunningdale, the Ryder Cup at Royal Lytham, Walton Heath and the Belfry, the PGA Championship and a crop of World Match–Play Championships with a variety of sponsors at Wentworth and, once, the Sun-Alliance Match–Play when it was staged at Stoke Poges in 1977. I was following the final pair, Brian Huggett and Hugh Baiocchi, when suddenly we were joined by Colin Cowdrey. 'I was watching cricket at the Parks,' he said, 'and I heard you on my radio. I thought it would be nice to cheer Brian [a close friend and also a business associate of 'Kipper's'] home so I drove down here.' Unfortunately for Colin, Baiocchi beat Huggett, but what a delight to be in the company of three of sport's most charming practioners at the end of the day. Oddly enough, one of my lasting memories of the occasion is of the birdsong in the trees when I heard the recording of my interview with Baiocchi and reflected on the marvellous tranquillity of the setting. Stoke Poges . . .

> Now fades the glimmering landscape on the sight,
> And all the air a solemn stillness holds,
> Save where the beetle wheels his droning flight,
> And drowsy tinklings lull the distant folds.

With very real regret I gave up golf commentary after the 1986 Open at Turnberry, but it had to be done. In 1985 I had been merely soaked at Prince's. The following year the weather in south-west Scotland was indescribable.

For the first time, I followed one particular player in every round of the Open and in all truth it seemed that only Greg Norman would be strong enough to fight the vile weather. I was delighted that his playing partner on the Saturday was Gordon J. Brand, that gritty Yorkshireman from Baildon, because it is rather pleasant to have a personal link, however tenuous, with one of the players one is following. Gordon J. Brand is a fellow

Yorkshireman and neither of us had ever needed to be reminded of that kinship, so on that July Saturday when the
heavens opened and the wind screamed in from the Firth of
Clyde there was an unspoken bond of mutual sympathy. Being
blown out to the far northern end of the course was bad enough;
when we turned to face the wind and rain on the twelfth it all
became just too much. It was like facing a Panzer Division, the
weather a wall of grey steel confronting us, defying anyone
by any means to penetrate it. While Gordon was playing his
second shot, Norman perched on the front of our buggy for a
moment and inquired, conversationally, if we were all insane to
be out there. It gave me food for thought. My wife told me later
that my next broadcast, from the twelfth fairway, caused her to
fall off her seat with laughter, so abject was the misery of our
condition reflected in my words and tone.

Every last square inch of my clothing was utterly saturated;
dampness swirled over my whole, shivering torso. My sodden
'waterproofs' had long since hoisted the flag of unconditional
surrender and were now flattened hard against me like a heavy
shroud. And there were another two hours of this to be endured.
From time to time I forced my thoughts away from these
personal discomforts to admire the way Messrs Norman and
Brand battled against utterly impossible odds. And, my, how
they battled; it was magnificent. And then my introspection
dragged me back to the prospect of that long wait at the end of it
all for the traffic out of Turnberry to clear sufficiently for me to
get back to my hotel in Ayr and into a hot bath. It would not
happen for at least three hours. In three months time I would (I
hoped) reach my sixty-third birthday. There was a lot I wanted
to do with my life yet, and getting double pneumonia was not
high on my list of priorities.

It was good to see Norman win the title the following day and
just as good to see Brand take second place. By now, in my mind,
we were comrades in adversity and it was right that we should
come home in marginally better weather. The players had struck
the right sort of heroic note for me, basking in their reflected glory,
to bow out. The following year I watched television coverage
of the last day at Muirfield and caught a glimpse of Chris Rea
squelching his way down the last hole. I knew exactly how he felt.

Spectators, and their attitude to tournament golf, tend to vary on a geographical basis, although there is no clearly defined pattern to this – at least, that is what I have found while threading my way through them, either on foot or in the buggy. It is axiomatic that something like 99.9 per cent of the people lining the fairways will be golfers themselves and therefore crowd behaviour is probably better than in any other spectator sport. The one exception to this rule is probably at what is now the Three-Stars event, which took over when the Bob Hope Classic ceased to be played in this country. In both these tournaments a fair proportion of the spectators was concerned primarily with getting close to the showbiz and other personalities, like Telly Savalas, Hal Linden, Howard Keel, Henry Cooper, Jimmy Tarbuck, Bruce Forsyth and the rest.

This must have made life difficult for the professional golfers because in the three Bob Hopes I covered as a commentator it was quite commonplace for the star-struck fans to be chattering, perhaps exchanging notes on the autographs they had collected or were hoping to collect, while the pro in the group was at the top of his backswing. While one cannot 'knock' any money-raising event for charity, the tournament pros often had my profound sympathy on these occasions. I remember watching Peter Oosterhuis waiting something like five minutes before being able to putt out on the eighteenth at Moor Park while Bob Hope entertained the crowd with an impromptu cabaret act. No one could criticise him for entering into the spirit of the tournament to which he had given his name and which in turn helped to raise a lot of money for deserving causes; at the same time, no golfer could fail to appreciate the additional problems this delay caused to the professional player.

One of these occasions actually caused me a few emotional problems which should never enter the realms of commentary. This was when Group Captain Sir Douglas Bader went out on the Saturday afternoon of a Bob Hope Classic, and as he clumped his way stoically up the hill of the first hole at Moor Park a small boy standing close to my buggy on the edge of the fairway asked his father, 'What's he famous for, Dad?' And as Dad attempted to explain the wonder of Douglas Bader's career in the RAF I felt a huge lump gather in my throat. My subsequent broadcast owed more to respect and admiration for the man than to any golf that I saw that day.

It was during a Bob Hope Classic at Moor Park that I had the only conversation I am ever likely to have with a Head of State, past or present. Ex-President Gerald Ford was a regular competitor in the event and when I went to record an interview with him on the practice-ground I was struck by the laxity of the security about him. His bodyguards had come all the way across the Atlantic to protect him, but when I explained to them that I wanted to record a chat they never checked the content of the case in which I was carrying the Uher recorder, nor did they ask for any credentials to establish that I was who I said I was. Either they regarded me at a glance as totally trustworthy, or totally harmless, or they were just pleasantly relaxed in the ambience of the golf tournament. But as life in high places has become sadly but progresively less secure, I have often reflected that I *might* have been a wrong-'un and that case *might* have contained a hand-gun, and then a pleasant and courteous ex-president would have been no more.

Mr Ford was, in fact, so pleasant that he suggested I call at Vail Golf Club in Colorado (where he lends his name to a tournament similar to the Bob Hope Classic) if I should visit that part of the USA. By sheer chance I was there the following Easter, but I could not find the course. It was under four feet of snow.

Crowds in Scotland tend to be slightly reserved, especially in relation to those in the North of England when the Open is played at Royal Lytham or Royal Birkdale. But my award for the most pleasant crowd has to go to the multitude which assembled at the Belfry for Europe's Ryder Cup victory in 1985. On the final afternoon we solved the problem of trying to keep up commentary on vital matches by using three reporters who started operations on the tenth tee. As each match ended, the commentator hurried back to the tenth ready to start over again with a new match. This caused much to-ing and fro-ing through the crowds lining the fairways and, to a man (and woman) the spectators were helpful and accommodating. I must confess, therefore, to a fair amount of annoyance when the United States team complained afterwards about those spectators. There was indeed some restive stirring amongst the crowd when American players who had finished their round went out to support their team-mates. With them went a substantial following of wives, and this gallery, standing in line, obscured the paying public's view of many vital shots on that final afternoon. The crowd had reason to complain – much more so than the Americans at the criticism of the spectators whose view they were obscuring. But it was a great day, just the same.

Royal Birkdale is remembered by thousands of fans who have trudged through the black dust which is churned up on sunny Open occasions there. Severe scrubbing of the feet is the first requirement when one returns to the hotel in the evening. Turnberry is notable for the traffic jams which occur when the crowds start to wend their way home in the evening. The A77 is the only main road to and from the course and so those who have not been lucky enough to get a room in the Turnberry Hotel itself, or in Girvan, a few miles to the south, face a very slow trek northwards towards Ayr. But I remember with great affection that in 1977 the local justices granted Girvan pubs an extension until 1 a.m. during the Open!

Before leaving this look at some aspects of media coverage of golf I would like to offer a modest but genuine tribute to the Association of Golf Writers. It will not have escaped the attention of golfing readers of British newspapers that the coverage of their game is presented in infinitely more dignified terms than that of other mass participant and spectator sports. This is not an accident. In a working lifetime in the communications media I have found no other branch of sportswriting which shows anything like the same affection and regard and, above all, *respect* for the game with which it is associated. The AGW has won for itself facilities and co-operation from the R and A, the PGA and from players and sponsors which are the envy of those whose duties are concerned with writing about other sports. That could not have been achieved if the Association had not in turn earned the respect of those organisations and individuals who co-operate so readily. Indeed, I believe that the members of the AGW would in fact *revolt* if their newspapers and magazines tried to adopt the policy of trivialisation and diminishment which, sadly, has had such a disastrous effect on other games.

Don: While the US Masters tournament in Augusta is one of the great occasions in world golf, and I have never been there, I cannot help feeling that the Open Championship is the greatest of them all. Perhaps this is partly tradition, partly patriotism, partly the marvellous sense of occasion that one experiences every July, but the Open has always seemed to me to be very special indeed. I've scuffed my way around five of the courses which have staged the Open in recent years, but usually out-of-season and with nothing more than half-a-crown at stake, so how about giving us a pro's-eye view of the courses?

Ian: *Royal Lytham and St Anne's* is a wonderful test of golf and a good venue with plenty of accommodation within easy reach, lots of parking facilities and plenty of room for the tented village (which has become more of a tented *city* in recent years). Its weakness as an Open venue, in my view, is that most of the out-of-bounds is down the right, especially on the first nine holes and with the prevailing wind behind, or partly right to left; you are hoping to shoot 32 or 33 on the front nine and to hold on through the back nine. There is, therefore, an imbalance in difficulty when you look at the course as a whole. If you are playing a nice, steady round and stand on the four-teenth tee at level par you are now facing five holes in which four are more than 400 yards in length, all either into the wind or with it blowing left to right. You can, in consequence, play perfectly well and finish 5, 5, 4, 5, 5 to shoot a 76 or 77 and your card is in ruins. In terms of playability, Lytham is very good, but I think the imbalance prevents it from being a great test.

Royal Troon has many of the characteristics of Lytham. You get a bit of a nice ride out on the prevailing wind (although not quite as straightforward as Lytham) and then you have a lot of holes over 400 yards into the wind and/or left to right. In terms of a championship test and in terms of a spectacle it is unnerving watching great players just hanging on to hold their scores together. I think Troon is perhaps the least popular of all the championship venues.

Royal Birkdale is my favourite, perhaps for personal reasons because it is close to home and I have played it a lot, but instead of playing over the sanddunes, as on many links courses, you play between them, so all the fairways are flat and all the holes are defined by the sandhills. It is a very attractive, slightly flattering, aesthetically pleasing golf course; even if you play it in the middle of winter without the stands and the crowds it still impresses you as a championship course because the huge dunes (on which so many spectators stand on tournament occasions) are ranged all around the greens. It is not the hardest of the Open courses to play but it is still a wonderful test of golf on which you have to use every club in the bag, and it has probably the best par-five in the world – the fifteenth. Downwind, it has the unique quality of being a great two-shotter requiring a very accurate tee-shot to the right of the three traps guarding the left side of the fairway, while on the right there is willow scrub and a ditch.

Going for the green in two, you have to go over the corner of the gorse, and carry a whole bunch of traps on to a green which is slightly angled. If it is playing into the wind (or with no wind) it is now a wonderful three-shotter because all the trouble is judiciously placed. To leave yourself with a medium third shot, you have to take a big chance with the second. It's a superb test because it makes you think so much. In the English Open of 1988, I worked out quite simply to play it in five – with a three-iron off the tee, a three-iron second and a five to the green. I got my five, which didn't improve the card, of course, but I really enjoyed it as an exercise in discipline, in planning and in course-management.

Muirfield is one of the most attractive courses. It doesn't knock all the life out of you, but it's hard. It has to be remembered, too, that there are tees on Open Championship courses which most golfers never see, and if you look at a course in the pages of a book and perhaps think it doesn't look *too* difficult, bear in mind that on Open occasions the holes are

designed to bring all the problems into play for top-class
players operating from the back tees. The sixth at Muirfield is a
hole which requires a lot of planning; there's a wonderful
par-three at the seventh and, along with Lytham, it provides an
exceptionally good finishing hole. When Faldo won the Open in
1987 he played the hole immaculately and traditionally winners have done – Nicklaus when he won in 1966, Trevino in
1972 and Watson in 1980. This is not to say that other courses
have not seen exciting finishes at the eighteenth, but I think
Lytham and Muirfield provide the classic finishing holes.

Turnberry is in some ways a strange course. I think the
definitive statement on it was made by Nicklaus after he had
played in those horrendous conditions in 1986 when he was
interviewed for BBC Radio by Roddy Forsyth. He said, 'We
came here in 1977 and two very good players played exceptionally well. All things considered, I think we had a very
successful Open. The next time we came to the same venue they
had changed the course completely.' The implication of what
he was saying was obvious and I think it was fair comment. On
that occasion the course was made to be just about as unplayable as any course I have ever seen.

You have angled tee-shots at Turnberry – the tees are not all
facing straight down the fairways, so you come into the fairways
from one side or the other. Consequently, if the wind gets up the
ball is moved across towards the rough. In 1986 the fairways
were extremely narrow and they had let the rough grow so
high that you couldn't even find your ball. In one respect they
were unlucky in that having set the course up like that, good
weather was essential – and Turnberry had the most spectacularly bad weather I have ever known in mid-summer. It was
icy cold, with strong winds, and it was raining. Father's experience of those conditions is reported elsewhere with great
feeling, so you can imagine what it was like trying to play in
them.

Forgetting for a moment that unfortunate Open, the course is
probably, after Birkdale, the most straightforward of the
venues. Most shots can be played from a level stance and
shot-making does not have to be too subtle or too varied. (I am,
of course, talking about players of the highest level – it is a very

good golf course.) But in the last analysis, the best asset of Turnberry is its scenic quality; it is not the best test.

Royal St George's is the most difficult; on a bad day it can be virtually unplayable. The greens often have huge undulations and some of them seem to have been designed not to accept any golf shot at all. I would defy anyone to come up with a game-plan to play the fourth if the wind is in the wrong quarter. I was playing a practice round before the 1985 Open and Mike Bonallack (secretary of the R and A) came out and stood on top of the sand-trap which lies in wait for the stray tee-shot at the fourth. At a guess, the top of that bunker is about thirty-five feet above the player who has found sand. Now, in a bunker shot, of course, you do hit the sand first with the blade wide open and cut across the ball to give you control and to impart spin. But doing this deprives the stroke of much of its momentum and there is a limit to how far you can hit an explosion shot. I tried, from the bottom of that trap, to play my shot straight ahead and unless I perched the ball on top of the sand, in a perfect lie, it was physically impossible to escape in a forward direction.

Mike Bonallack was watching this and I said to him, 'If we get a head wind here in the morning, unless the tee is set a little bit forward it is going to be impossible to clear the trap, and with only about five yards of fairway to the left of the trap before you come to deep rough, we are going to have trouble. There will be a succession of players going into this trap and when it gets a bit chewed up no one is going to be able to get out.' He had a look at it all and I am sure he was conscious of the problem. Remember, we have so far looked only at the first half of a hole of something like 440 yards and the second half is almost as hard. The green is placed on a ridge with a huge valley on the left front and, as everything slips off the right side there are so many ways of making six and seven it just isn't true.

There are many other tricky holes and the one which stands out in my mind is the eighteenth. A ridge runs down the centre of the fairway, and as the tee is set to the right of the fairway you are attacking the ridge at an angle. If you drive with a bit of draw, and the ball catches the off-side of the ridge, it kicks away into the left-hand rough and you can't get up from there. If you play it defensively from the tee with a bit of a fade and it catches the other side of the ridge, it dribbles away into the right-hand semi-rough where you cannot see the green. If by some miracle you negotiate your ball on to the fairway, you are left with a shot of over 200 yards with a little pot bunker guarding the right side of the green; if you go left of the tiny neck of country leading into the green you are down in a valley where all the water gathers. I must have looked at that hole probably sixty or seventy times and I still have no idea how to play it.

(**Don:** Ian's view of Sandwich might perhaps be a little jaundiced after an experience on the neighbouring Prince's course while pre-qualifying for the 1985 Open at Royal St George's. He was bitten by a spider! Possibly his apprehension at seeing two punctures on his right hand, after brushing the spider away, was enhanced by a recent trip to Australia where funnel-webs, and their antipodean arachnidan kin, pose a generally more unpleasant threat than anything usually found on the seashores of Kent. Anyway, the incident earned him the distinction of featuring in a Roy Ulyett cartoon in the *Daily Express*.)

St Andrews is everything people imagine it to be and by 'people' I suppose I mean everyone who has ever played golf. It must be the ambition of every player to have a round at the world headquarters of the game. At first glance, the Old Course looks like nothing on earth; it takes a long time to get to like it and a lifetime to understand it. Nearly all the fairways are shared and nearly all the greens as well; you go out down the right-hand side, cross over for the loop of holes seven, eight, nine, ten and eleven, and then come back on the right-hand side, so all the danger – scrub or out-of-bounds – is on the right for most of the way. Therefore, if you are playing a round simply for pleasure you keep the ball left, and so long as you avoid the bunkers, you are in play, and with those huge double greens you have plenty of target to aim at. The marvellous subtlety of the course, however, lies in the realisation that if you have hit the ball to the left, off the tee, and if you have avoided the traps, the ball now seems to be kicking away from the hole all the time.

There now seems always to be a little knoll, or ridge, or hummock, or an angle of the green, or a trap which compels you to approach the green at an angle which makes the ball run away from the hole. Consequently, you tend to end up forty or fifty or even sixty feet away from the hole, and no one is going to get down in two putts from that distance on all eighteen holes. If you are more brave off the tee – although it looks like insanity as you stand there surveying all the trouble on the right and all those wide open spaces on the left – suddenly you realise that this is where you should be: the second shot can be angled in around a small hill, or there *is* a route past the trap, or there is a little bit of flat green to run the ball through. This is when you begin to appreciate the enormous cleverness of it all and the need to play the course properly is brought home to you. And as you approach the end of it you then come to that great seventeenth hole. It forces you to do what you don't want to do. You know that the second shot has to be played from as far right as possible, but as you stand on the tee all you can see is the hotel and the new building on the corner. If you don't nail the tee-shot, you don't carry the obstruction. If you get the ball into a prime position and consider, now, that fiendishly difficult green, there is actually no way to get the ball within ten feet of the flag when it is in an Open Championship position.

Golfers *hate* accepting defeat; they find it difficult to accept that there is no way of getting the ball close. So they are always tempted to flirt too dangerously with the bunker. There are three certain recipes for disaster on the seventeenth: one is to go out of bounds off the tee; next, you can get into the bunker and have a bad lie (televiewers have seen Brian Barnes take six bunker shots there, Tommy Nakajima take six, Mark Mouland take six, and that doesn't count all the people viewers *haven't* seen come to grief in this fashion); and the third way is to go over the green on to the road. The surface of the road has changed over the years. It used to be loose shale, and with the ball lying between bits of flint and rubble it was virtually impossible to get it on to the green and stop it. Now you have the wall, a little green belt, the tarmac road, a small uneven walkway and then a steep grassy bank and there is really no shot which will go through all these different surfaces with a reasonable measure of control. You are looking at double bogey if you go through on to the road. That is why the seventeenth does now rate amongst tournament players as the hardest and most dangerous hole around. Then you come to the eighteenth.

Don: Surely there is nothing complicated about the eighteenth at St Andrews? I have only played the course once but I had a par-four at the last, so it has got to be a straightforward hole.

Ian: I think perhaps it would be best if (with respect) you simply treasured the memory of that four and never played the course again, because I would regard another par score at the last hole as highly improbable. Here you are faced with several acres of well-kept grass with no obstacles on it, but there is a classic way of making a bogey five. That is to fire into the wide open spaces of the adjoining first and eighteenth fairways, basically aiming at the steps of the clubhouse. That now leaves you with the Valley of Sin directly between you and the pin. It is difficult to visualise a mere two putts from the bottom of the Valley so you have to make sure of getting over it. That can take you to the back of the green, and even thirty-five feet past the flag is enough to give you the most subtle and unreadable putt that you will find anywhere in golf. Henry Longhurst, I remember, forecast that Doug Sanders in 1970 was going to leak his three-foot putt to win the Open out on to the right lip. His words, as I remember them, were, 'It is the side you are always going to go,' or something like that, and it was quite right. Those with experience of the green – and those who were not being asked to hole that particular putt – knew that it was an inside-left-lip putt. From where Sanders, with putter in hand, was standing, it looked to be inside-*right*-lip. It had to be. The first putt for anyone who has played to the back of the green, the long one, looks like straight downhill at lightning speed, but there are two huge sweeping breaks on that green which are far from obvious as you stand over the ball – a hole of unbelievable subtlety and challenge.

13 The Spirit of the Tour

Don: At first glance it seems remarkable that there is such a marked degree of mutual assistance between pairs of players, and even groups of them, in what is, after all, a highly individual game. One would expect to see cut-throat competition, intense rivalry; instead, we find one player going out of his way to help another who might be having problems of one form or another.

Ian: Exactly. Can you think of another game where two competitors are practising alongside each other before going out to play for a lot of money; one asks the help of the other because his swing is not right or he is not lining up his putts correctly, for instance? Only the tiniest fraction of golfers on the circuit would jib at giving a hand. To the outside world it might appear unusual; on the circuit it is commonplace, the sort of thing we take for granted. The competition is not so much one individual against another as the pair of them against *the course*.

Don: So it is possible for close friendships to develop on the tour between players who are in daily competition – against the course if you like, but still there is prize money at stake, which must make it a personal duel in some respects?

Ian: Some of my closest relationships are with guys I have been playing with since our amateur days. For instance, I first met Warren Humphreys when we were paired together in the Boys' International, in 1967. Although slightly younger than me, Warren was already established as one of the outstanding talents in amateur golf. He came from a very much more 'fasionable' club, Royal Mid-Surrey, than mine and was already, at sixteen, much more experienced than me in amateur golf circles, He was, I suppose, more sophisticated, too, and he set out straightaway to make me feel more comfortable in my first major competitive event. On the first tee he asked, 'Are you feeling nervous?' and when I replied, 'Yes,' he responded, 'So am I.' If it all sounds very basic now, it went a long way towards making me feel better at the time.

I was vaguely aware of some sort of north–south divide in those days. It wasn't a big thing but quite a lot of us had grown up together in Lancashire junior golf and there was a sort of them-and-us situation when we came up against boys from the bigger, wealthier and more renowned clubs of the south. So I suppose I expected almost anything from this young man from the stockbroker belt except this relaxed and friendly approach. We roomed together at the Prince of Wales Hotel in Southport during the full internationals of 1971 and we met frequently on the amateur circuit at events like the Brabazon, the Golf Illustrated Gold Vase, the Lytham Trophy, the Berkshire and the English and British championships. When he first turned professional, Warren's travelling companion was Roddy Carr, son of the famous Joe, and it was after Roddy retired from the circuit that Warren and I started to travel abroad together and to stay at each other's homes for tournaments in this country when it was convenient to do so. But before this happened I was present at, and a witness to, an incident which is now part of the folklore of golf and which many people have found it difficult to believe. We were practising alongside each other for the 1970 Open at St Andrews when Jack Nicklaus approached. He said to Warren, 'My name is Nicklaus. I understand we are playing together tomorrow so I just wanted to say "Hello" and that I am looking forward to it.' Nicklaus at that time was the greatest golfer in the world; Warren was an eighteen-year-old amateur player. But it happened. I saw and heard it, a little over-whelmed by it all.

Don: Ian used to return from his early days in Europe chafing at the loneliness of his evenings while he was away. Travel, the opportunity to see new places, has always been one of the great delights of my own working life, so I found it difficult to understand why he didn't take the opportunity to explore some of the places he visited in more detail. I am still staggered, for instance, by the thought that in all his visits to Madrid he has never thought of visiting the Prado. Different tastes, I suppose.

Ian: That has never appealed to me, I'm afraid, and eve-

nings in European cities did tend to be boring and tedious. That
was when Warren and I decided to invest in a video-recorder
and power-pack. The original idea was to film ourselves and
analyse our swings and the video was used for that purpose
exclusively until we discovered the cassettes of Shell's *Wonderful
World of Golf*. We spent hours watching them at Warren's home
while playing in the south and gradually we began to think,
'Wouldn't it be great if we could do this in Europe where the
television programmes were incomprehensible to us?'

We could not only watch golf films but we could hire, or buy,
other cassettes to keep ourselves entertained. So off we went to
the French Open and spent three hours in our hotel room –
trying to play English cassettes through a French television set!
No, we weren't very worldly-wise or technically accomplished
in those days. It never occurred to us that French TV worked
on a different frequency. We had the back off the set and
virtually demolished the entire apparatus in our efforts to get a
picture on the screen. All in vain. There was nothing for it but to
acquire our own TV and take that as well; I found a small,
portable, black-and-white set.

Now, it's one thing taking this sort of gear on to the continent
when travelling by car; it's something else again when going by
air. But for ten years we never faltered, never thought about the
inconvenience, never failed to sally forth equipped for our own
in-house movie show. In doing so we broke just about every rule
in the book and deprived a whole series of airlines of the excess
baggage charges they might have levied. Such transgressions
were not achieved, I should add, without a good deal of effort on
our part.

We had a couple of Burberry holdalls, souvenirs of the Bob
Hope Classic where an assortment of such goodies were dispensed, and the video just fitted into one, while the portable TV
went into the other. The old Ferguson recorder, however,
weighed something like eighty or sixty pounds, and transporting it along those never-ending corridors at Heathrow was a
two-man job. We evolved a system of shoulder-straps, which
helped, a little, but the main problem lay in arriving at the
check-in desk, wearing expressions of serene innocence and
swinging the 'hand luggage' around as though it contained

nothing heavier than the regulation nightie and toothbrush. The tournament golf bag, plus suitcase (containing anything up to thirty video tapes!) disappeared into the hold of the aircraft while the Burberry holdalls sat smugly at our feet, waiting to be transported into the cabin with us. The combined weight of our respective burdens must have been nearer 150 pounds than the forty-four decreed by the regulations. We must have risked back-strain, putting out our shoulders and even affecting the trim of the aeroplane on so many trips into Europe. I fear that all these risks had to be taken in order to avoid the boredom of long continental evenings, and I am glad to say we never paid one penny in excess baggage charges.

Warren quit the tournament circuit after the 1987 season. We had had around ten good years of travelling together and a golfing friendship which stretched back more than twenty years. As he moved into a peripheral business side of the game it has meant that this can continue, though I miss his good companionship on the European tour – and his help in carrying the TV equipment! It has meant, however, that I am becoming more isolated as one of the veterans of the tour and survivors of the 1970s sub-culture.

Don: We have talked elsewhere about Celebrity Am–Am tournaments and the odd one in which I have been mad to become involved. These are great days for the amateur, even though they can be nerve-racking, but how do professionals regard this sort of round?

Ian: Pro–ams can be good little earners on non-tournament days, and they can be extremely useful in making contact with people one would never otherwise expect to meet. They can also prove interesting in all sorts of different ways. The first one I played in South Africa was on my first visit there. I was given an 'unknown' team, as befitted my novice status on the Sunshine tour, on a typical Johannesburg day – steamy hot with no hint of immediate trouble but a big electrical storm in the offing. My team included an international shot-putter who had never previously been on a golf course! He had done some work on a driving range and had been given a handicap of twenty-four for the tournament; he said he knew how to hit the ball. I was a little dubious about this, but I wasn't there to harbour doubts about my partners. The other two members of the four were an eccentric character who wasn't really a good player at all and a 'wily' player off twelve who made lots of pars and provided the solid backbone of the team. But the shot-putter was the secret weapon, as I quickly found out when he made a two at the first hole (a par-four of just over 400 yards) and he received two strokes there – he had started with a net nothing!

We soon had a miraculous score in prospect and all went well until the seventeenth hole, where we all came unstuck. I was heading for a bogey, which meant just one point in the Stableford scoring system; the shot-putter was way out of it; the wily one, for once, was not going to score; but suddenly the Eccentric fluked the ball on to the green for two. (He had become the Eccentric in my mind as soon as I set eyes on him. He was very tall and cadaverous-looking. His clothing was weird and he looked somewhere between an undertaker and a scarecrow.) He had scarcely uttered a word all the way round and it now occurred to me that we hadn't seen him putt at a single hole so far. If there hadn't been quite a bit of money at stake, precious indeed to me, I would have found what happened next excruciatingly funny. As it was, money or not, I found it difficult not to collapse in a fit of laughter.

With two putts for three Stableford points, Mr Eccentric lagged it up to about two and a half feet and then walked across to me. 'While the rest of my game is okay, I had better explain about my putting,' he said. 'A few years ago I had the yips something terrible and I had to find a way to cure it because it was ruining my golf. It might look a bit odd to you but I think it's the answer to my problems.' In point of fact, his game was little short of terrible and that should have given me the message, but I still wasn't prepared for what came next. He started to assemble the oddest putting stance I have ever seen, before or since, starting by standing facing *away* from the hole! He had the putter out to the side, and somehow wound the other arm across his chest and twisted it at an angle. It was an amazing sight. To cut a long and painful story short, he never did actually hole out from those two and a half feet. If we hadn't dragged him off the green he would probably still be there trying to get the ball into the hole.

The first Bob Hope Classic, at the RAC Club at Epsom was an innovation in that we were playing for Order of Merit points, it counted in Ryder Cup qualifying points – and we were playing with amateurs. I have a poignant memory of that because my friend, Warren Humphreys, from being dead and buried as far as the money-list was concerned – and he was having all kinds of problems with his game at the time – suddenly had a marvellous run towards the end of the season and got into the Bob Hope when he hadn't expected to do so. He now needed a good finish to get into the top sixty and thus into the exempt list for the following season. After shooting a couple of 67s he was playing the last needing a four, virtually for his immediate future. He was just short of the green in two, played a chip-and-run to about five feet and now he needed that putt, oh so badly. But he was playing with Bruce Forsyth, who saw it as his duty to entertain the crowd, just as father saw Bob Hope do later at Moor Park when Peter Oosterhuis was waiting to putt. He went through a routine which no doubt delighted his fans in the crowd – and when it had finished Warren missed his putt. That just about summed up what is wrong with counting that sort of contest as a tour event.

In one round of that first Bob Hope Classic my celebrity was George Savalas, brother of Telly, who played the part of Stavros in 'Kojak'. He weighed around twenty stones so they gave him an electric buggy to get him round and I suppose I should have seen the danger signals when he arrived with a carton of beer and another of Marlborough cigarettes, which he chain-smoked around the course while alternately swigging the beer. As a golfer he was quite simply a hacker, but that is not of great importance in a pro–am. What is important is that your partner follows the etiquette of the game and has some under-standing, some feel for it. Mr Savalas had none of that. On the tenth he drove his buggy over my ball, crunching it comprehen-sively into the ground; on another hole he parked directly in line between my pitch to the green and the flag, and he regularly abandoned it in a place which was directly behind the line of a putt. George was clearly under the impression that the crowds had come to Epsom to see him and no one else mattered.

Don: This sort of thing can work both ways, you know. I had enormous problems playing behind William Roache (Ken Barlow in 'Coronation Street') in an am–am for Clive Lloyd's Benefit before he retired as a Lancashire cricketer.

Ian: Bill's a mate of mine – he's a good chap.

Don: I know, that's why I'm making this point. He was a relatively late starter in the game and the bug obviously bit him very badly. He played this 'fun' am–am as though he were competing in the final round of the Open: three or four practice-swings before every shot, then he would stand admiring his effort and/or play the shot in retrospect; he stalked every putt on every green from every angle; he consistently left his clubs on the 'wrong' side of every green so there was yet another delay when he had finally holed out. The field was very quickly stacked up behind us. Immediately following me was Frank Myler, a Rugby League international player and then a manager, who was an accomplished golfer with, quite rightly, little time for those who played without regard for others on the course. Next behind him came 'Flat' Jack Simmons, who became increasingly colourful in expressing his concern at the delay, and behind him there was a whole gaggle of Lancashire cricketers. When we reached a short hole there would be as many as sixteen players in the queue, all singing hymns of hate against Mr Barlow in particular and 'Coronation Street' in general.

Then, dammit, he caused congestion on the practice green when we tried to play an eighteen-hole putting competition. While you play as well as you can, pro–ams and am–ams should be about fun, and a laugh, and enjoyment, and making new friends. They certainly shouldn't be about going home in a thoroughly bad temper.

Ian: Agreed, absolutely. In contrast to George Savalas, I played one round in that first Bob Hope Classic with a chap called Lee Harrigan who was the European attorney for Coca-Cola. He had already played one round with Sam Snead as his pro and Sam – a legendary figure in world golf but a notoriously bad pro–am participant – had given him a very hard day indeed. I set out to treat him with the same courtesy that I hope I accord my partners in all such events and we had a thoroughly pleasant day.

In other pro–ams I have played with Shaking Stevens, who turned out to be an extremely quiet, almost shy, person. Feeling that he might want to get away from the showbiz atmosphere for a day, I asked what I should call him. He replied, 'Oh, just "Shaky".' He clearly had a special appeal to very young fans and we played with an entourage of fourteen and fifteen-year-olds wearing badges which proclaimed, 'I Love Shaky', and they screamed and shouted every time he hit the ball.

Michael Parkinson – well, he's a friend of father's so I had to expect him to be good news, and indeed I had an extremely pleasant round. I enjoyed his dry humour, his love of cricket and his company generally. Another television personality in the same mould was Henry Kelly. His natural characteristics are those he portrays on TV, and since he is fanatical about cricket and horse-racing we found plenty to talk about. Robert Powell, the actor, is another cricket fan and a fascinating companion, and all these chaps tend to bring 'Test Match Special' into the conversation. I have played with Alec Bedser in the ATS pro–am at Stoke Poges, and on meeting on the first tee watched my hand disappear into his huge one just about all the way to the elbow. I have had a pleasant clubhouse conversation with Cliff Thorburn, the snooker player, and played in a Bob Hope Classic with Russ Abbott, who conforms to the classic comedian's character by being very quiet when he's away from his 'Madhouse' idiom. Mandy and I had dinner with Russ and Mrs Abbott and it was pleasant, if a little surprising, to find that he was nothing like his TV image – apart from being able to get a table immediately, in a crowded restaurant!

Jimmy Tarbuck is one of my favourite people, both as a golfer and a comedian. He is a genuinely funny man off the stage as well as on it, but on a golf course he's a very serious player who goes out a lot with pros and is used to it. Consequently he has a complete 'feel' for the game and its etiquette. He is also a very good golfer – in the Four Stars tournament he eagled the last while I was making six, so I could have used his card there.

Richie Benaud is one of the best I have ever played with. On the first tee we talked cricket (and relatives!) and then he said, 'As a professional sportsman, I think I know what's required out here. You tell me what you want from me and I'll do my best to help.' I have played with Tony Dali and some years ago I used to play a lot with the 'Coronation Street' crowd – Alan Browning when he was married to Patricia Phoenix ('Elsie Tanner'), who used to wait for him after the round; with Graham Haberfield, and with Bill Roache. We are still pals, despite father's experience with him! Eric Sykes is a great man to play with, very dry and extremely witty, but, being deaf, he can switch off his hearing-aid and retreat into his own little world. Everybody seems to like Eric Sykes, whether it is in golf or show business.

One of the most interesting partners I have had is Tom Courtenay, the actor. We played together in Jersey and before we went out Alan Price, the singer, said to me, 'Just make sure you look after Tom because he's a bit "down".' It was shortly after his film *The Dresser* had been up for an award and then didn't get it. The offers of parts which had been expected after the success of the film had not materialised and Alan said they had brought Tom over for the golf to try to cheer him up a bit. So I suppose that of all the tour pros he might have drawn for the pro–am, he had got one of the keenest movie-buffs. We went out to the practice ground and I gave him a bit of coaching, then started talking about his films. He told me about making *One Day in the Life of Ivan Denisovitch*, that gruelling, down-beat Russian film which was made somewhere up near the Arctic Circle in unbelievably arduous conditions; the story was fascinating. I grew up with films like *Billy Liar*, *The Loneliness of the Long-Distance Runner* and I loved Tom's work in *King Rat*, so all in all it helped bring him out of himself a bit and for me it was great to be able to chat to a man whose work I admired.

Don: Sixteen years is not an inordinately long period of time and the changes you have seen during your professional career must seem quite startling – from the conditions of playing the tour to the equipment you use?

Ian: That's right. I suppose many of the youngsters now joining the tour imagine that it was always like this: beautifully organised tournaments with one's every need catered for; absolutely top-notch clubs and balls, so good that you find yourself wondering how their quality can ever be improved and yet you know that someone, somewhere, is beavering away to produce even higher standards. I started with a half-set provided by my first teacher and then I got a full set through a mail order firm of Spalding Cro-flites, lovingly acquired, club by club. The heads – as seemed to be common at that time – were screwed on and lightly glued. They started to unscrew when I practised a lot, but I persevered with them for a couple of years and then turned to a Nicklaus set with quite a decent blade.

When I turned pro I was looking for 'a deal' with one of the big manufacturers of clubs and balls and I had an interview with Dunlop, but my timing was unfortunate. Dunlop had decided on a change of policy in the early seventies and withdrew their sponsorship of a fairly big group of young, promising hopefuls in favour of putting their money behind a much smaller number of top-flight pros. So I went to Uniroyal, who were trying to get into the golf market, and they were generous and easy-going about it all. They provided clubs and a big bag of practice-balls, which at that time seemed riches untold, so soon (it seemed) after I had roamed the rough of Denton golf club looked for new treasures to supplement my supply of golf balls. With a new set of clubs and a smart bag and what seemed to be an unlimited supply of balls, I felt great. Unfortunately, the clubs were made on the same principle as my first set – screwed and lightly glued – so that in my first winter in South Africa the glue started to soften and the heads to turn slightly. The heads of my six- and nine-irons came right off while I was actually playing and I played the remainder of the tour with two clubs missing from my bag! Fourteen years later that sounds utterly incredible; at the time, if it was not exactly commonplace, it was, nevertheless, a vicissitude I simply had to cope with. After all, the previous year, my driver had broken in La Manga and I simply played on without it. Unimaginable today.

It was all part of a terrible naïvety on my part, but the first time I became aware that there were very different types of covers on golf balls was when I played a practice round for the 1974 Open with three Americans – Forrest Fesler, John Mahaffey and Hubert Green. (In those days I loved the glamour of playing alongside the big names and put my name down on the starting sheet with the best-known players I could find.) One of them looked at a Uniroyal ball with which I was playing and said, 'I haven't seen one of these before. Is it a Syrlin cover?' It was, but at that time I hadn't the faintest idea what he was talking about. Only a couple of years later did I get some real indication about the way golf balls can vary. My friend Eddie Birchenough, formerly pro at Denton, had moved to Gog Magog in Cambridgeshire and he took me to Great Shelford and introduced me to the Wheeler brothers, Barrie and Tony, who ran Shelford Engineering.

Barrie, who was to become a great friend, is the man who invented the cricket bat with the scooped-out back which was to become so popular with some first-class players. The way this came about was that he liked the principle of the large 'sweet spot' on Ping golf clubs (the big selling point with Ping putters) and he wanted to see if the principle could be applied to other sporting equipment. In his office he had all kinds of original golf equipment, including a putter with a grip about two inches thick. This enabled Barrie to prove, by some principle of physics, that a large grip reduced the rotation of the clubhead and therefore produced a squarer blade. (At the same time it took away the 'feel' of the club so it didn't work, but it is just another illustration of the working of an inquiring mind.) Barrie loves experimenting. At our first meeting he asked if I knew much about golf balls and I was able to answer with perfect truth, 'No. Nothing at all.' So he invited me to pay a visit when we had more time and to bring along a dozen balls of the type I used on the circuit. That was when I discovered the difference between Syrlin and Ballata covers, but first Barrie applied a ring-gauge to the balls I had brought along, which very quickly established that out of those twelve, I had one that went through, two which would not pass through at all and nine which were egg-shaped and could be twisted through at different angles. And these were golf balls with which I was trying to play tournament golf!

Next, we cut through the Syrlin cover and found that it was twice as thick on one side in nearly every case as it was on the other. We then turned to the Titleist balls, with Ballata covers, and a random selection, when checked, proved to be a precise

1.68 inches and perfectly round. The Syrlin cover is a silicone compound plastic, very tough and cut-resistant, but because it is so hard it does not compress against the clubface; you get a smaller striking area and can impart less spin. So if you are not a top-class player and you don't know (or care) how the ball is going to spin, you have a durable, non-spinning, long-lasting ball which seems to go further because it 'jumps' off the clubface. Consequently, it is a big-selling golf ball to the average club player. Professionals use the Ballata case, which is a rubber compound and cuts very easily because it is a thin cover, and that's why we use lots of balls in a single round. My final round in the Monte Carlo Open was an obvious exception to the rule, but that had nothing to do with the composition of the product. Bernhard Langer used to use as many as eighteen balls in a single round before the rules were altered slightly in 1987.

It seems light-years since I was hunting for golf balls at Denton and then pleading with companies to give me a ball-contract on the professional circuit when I look at things as they are today. Fifteen years ago I was happy simply to have enough balls to play during the season. Dunlop and Titleist are the companies vying to produce the most popular ball with pro-fessionals – they produce about the two best Ballata balls – and they have reps at all the tournaments who make sure you get supplies. You don't have to go looking for them; the reps find you and hand over the week's quota of ammunition. There is even a cash bonus for performance with a particular golf ball. I think Titleist are slightly better, but it's perhaps an arguable point. But to think that there's a bonus available for playing the ball you would want to be using in the first place – it's almost frightening. Oh yes. Things have changed.

On the tour now we have the Mizuno caravan, which can work miracles of club repair *on the spot*. This is fronted by Barrie Willett, one of the most respected clubmakers and repairers in Britain, with one admin man and three whiz-kids whom we've timed at work. A grip takes a matter of seconds, a shaft a couple of minutes and they can do a full set in half an hour. They have all the equipment in the mobile workshop, and just about any repair or adjustment which is necessary can be carried out in an incredibly short time. As far as clubs themselves are concerned, there have been three real innovations in the time I have been playing, because the fads of aluminium, titanium and early graphite all passed without making an effective challenge to steel. Now we have the upgraded graphite, the best being the XR gold, from Mizuno. I have one of those shafts in my driver, and when you try it before it has been made into a club the shaft has almost no discernible weight at all. Yet I have the No. 11 XR gold pushed through the clubhead and it has the flex of an X 400 or 500 but no weight at all, so I can weight the head up and have it swinging heavier, or I can have an overall light club – there is so much choice.

That shaft is, I would say, the biggest improvement. Next, the metal-headed wood, which in my opinion does not send the ball any further. The great advantage is that they are made out of a mould, so that once the manufacturers have got the head right (and the three or four firms who make them *have* got it right) they can keep on pulling out the heads from the mould and they are all as good as each other, whereas in the old days, with a persimmon wooden-headed driver, even when the head was nearly ready it had to be bored, and the way the bore went in dictated the angle of the shaft. Some were good, some were bad, but by the time the club was made there was nothing further you could do about it. So I think the metal-headed drivers are as good (though no better), but because they are so durable and easy to repeat they are very useful indeed – a bit like disposable nappies. Rather than having one favourite old driver, you can go and get them repaired any time. Perhaps the most important shot-saving, golf-improving development has been square grooves on the blade. These enable us in effect to bite into the cover of the ball, hold it on the club face, impart more spin and so give us more control of the flight, and because we don't mind cutting up the balls and tearing them up that has been one of the biggest innovations during my time on the circuit.

Don: So much for new equipment, but there have been other developments which have helped towards improved scoring, haven't there?

Ian: I think Ian Wright must come into the story at this point

– the man who provides some of us, at any rate, with detailed charts of every hole on any particular course and more details of pin positions which, of course, change each day. He started this about three years ago and carried on despite being taken up as Sevvy Ballesteros's caddie in 1988, and I am delighted to say he is going to carry on doing it. To me Ian's work is especially valuable because it removes the need to do 'paperwork' during a practice round. This has always been the least interesting part of tournament golf as far as I am concerned. You are on the course where you are going to be playing in real earnest either the following day or the one after that when you will be highly stimulated. Consequently, in the practice round you feel flat; you go through the motions but you do it without any adrenalin flowing. But at the same time you have to work out the shots which are going to be necessary in the tournament itself so you can neither relax completely and make it a sort of social round, nor can you derive the professional satisfaction which comes from a good work-out on the practice ground. So you make the best of it in any way you can.

Some guys like to have a bet – I have never done that because I am so flat that I would always lose and Yorkshiremen, of course, only like to bet on certainties. You can pass some of the time by working out the yardages, but now the PGA have coloured dots marked at intervals on the fairway it is possible to get a very accurate picture of each hole. This is where Ian Wright comes in. He goes out at the crack of dawn, comes back and draws eighteen sketch-maps showing the distances involved, the traps, trees, water hazards and the positioning of the flags. A couple of years ago Ian was a caddie known as 'Two Bags', because he always seemed to work for a player who missed the cut and then had to try to find another bag to carry in the final two rounds. He supplemented his income by preparing these maps, and he has about thirty clients who pay him a fixed fee per week throughout the season. It's the sort of enterprise which ought to be encouraged. Ian has found someone to photocopy his plans and someone else who staples them together in a little booklet. It makes a pleasant change from having to lug around our own pedometers from one tournament to another.

Don: To what extent do you rely on these yardages, which have been calculated in advance, rather than basing your estimates on a personal, visual assessment.

Ian: I can speak only for myself, you understand, but now that they are so accurate, now that I have got a set of golf clubs with square grooves and the lofts and lies are regularly checked, now that we play with very good golf balls which do not have variation in flight and distance, I rely somewhere between 80 and 90 per cent on yardages. I learned the game working totally on visual estimates, so it has been a long process. To let go of your natural inclination to play the shot as the eye tells you to play it is a difficult thing, but trial and error finally forces you to a simple conclusion: the book does not lie, while the eye *can* deceive.

I suppose the extent to which the tour has changed for the better was most forcibly brought home to me at the Volvo Masters at Valderrama towards the end of 1988. A courtesy car was available to every player; a players' marquee was sited on the edge of the practice ground with free food for everyone; there was an immaculate practice area; and when you arrived a bucket of new Titleist golf balls, with your name on it, was handed to you – no queueing! There was a locker with your name on it, a lounge facility within the locker-room with sandwiches and fresh fruit – absolutely every attention had been paid to the last possible detail of any player's requirements. I stood amidst these trappings of luxury and my mind went back to the Madrid Open at Real Club Deportivo Las Lomas-El Bosque in 1975, which was about an hour from the Don Quixote hotel in the town centre, where everyone was staying. A bus picked us up in what seemed the middle of the night, in pitch darkness, to take us to the course. It was still dark when we arrived and the clubhouse was locked up! Eventually, some sort of janitor arrived, minutes before the first players were due to tee off. A cup of coffee? We must be joking. And since there was only one bus back at night, we were stuck there for the whole day, irrespective of our starting times, with no facilities whatsoever.

I thought about La Manga – palatial though it may be today – where we played the Spanish Open for six years in a row from 1973. Clearly there were plans for the massive development that one sees today, but fifteen years ago it was like a scene from an American Western: tumbleweed blowing across a bare strip of sand and very little else to delight to the eye. Again there was only one bus and you were marooned at the course for the day, which was a considerable factor in terms of one's game. When you are playing under a certain amount of stress it is very necessary to have facilities for relaxation and to indulge in some form of escapism. I remember buying some bread and cheese and fruit in a supermarket to eat after my round at La Manga and getting a blast from the locker-room attendant. Oh yes, indeed–everything has changed. And very much for the better. The Volvo tournament of 1988 served to underline just how far the tour has progressed. At the risk of sounding like an old-timer I just hope young players joining the tour today realise that.

At the same time, the cost of playing the circuit has increased dramatically, so that it now can cost around £1,000 a week to take part in the more distant tournaments in Europe and around £700 for the nearer ones. For the Scandinavian Open, for instance, even through a tour-operator, flight and hotel costs would be £370, shuttle connection to Heathrow £120, caddie costs £250 to £300, an evening meal in Stockholm between £20 and £30 – so you are heavily into big spending before you can think of a drink or a night out. For the 1972 Open at Muirfield, Andrew Chandler, Ian Gradwell and myself went up in a Hillman Imp (petrol about five bob a gallon and the Imp didn't use much). Right at the last minute we found a three-bedded room in the home of a young couple for 17s 6d a night (87½p) and a huge breakfast. We caddied for ourselves and even got a few free golf balls – simply because it was the Open. With a fish supper in the evening for less than half a crown, and sharing the cost of petrol, we thus spent seven or eight nights there (we had to pre-qualify, of course) and still had change out of £20!

Every young man joining the tour today will expect to have a bonus on his club-contract, a bonus for playing particular golf balls and clubs, probably an extra bonus for having his bag sign-written plus whatever he can get from off-the-course sources; he will regard it as the norm to have courtesy cars available and to have food of good quality and variety available free of charge; he will almost certainly have his own car to get

around Europe and he will expect to stay in high-class accommodation. I note these changes without envy; I just hope
today's young pros realise that it was not always like this and
that an awful lot of work, notably by the PGA European Tour
Committee and PGA Tour Enterprises Ltd, its business arm,
has gone into achieving these conditions.

They have, of course, manifested themselves in greatly improved standards of play, which are most obvious at the top
level because Europe can now win the Ryder Cup and British
players can win the Open Championship. The Americans come
over to take part in the World Match-Play Championship, and
instead of seeing a token British player who we used to know
was going to be beaten in the first round we now almost
sympathise with the US players because we know they are not
going to reach the final these days. On the other hand, for us
journeymen this improvement has meant the lowering of 'cut'
scores. Top players don't have to worry about that because they
are so much better and the cut does not normally affect them.
But the broad mass of European tour players have to make the
cut and have to make a cheque of some kind every week. Theirs
is not a life of wondering how close they are to the top of the
money-winners' list; it is simply about making a living. In the
early seventies, if we were playing a difficult course, the cut
would be anything from 151 to 155 and on an easier course it
would be 148-ish. Now, if we play anything remotely like a
straightforward course and it's soft and a little bit damp, the cut
is one, two or three under par. Similarly, if we play a more
difficult course, the figure still comes down pro rata. For
instance, in the Laurence Batley at Royal Birkdale in 1987, the
cut was 145 − 145 at Birkdale! That would have won the
tournament when I was starting on the circuit. But, as I have
said, the facilities now are good for *all* the players. I saw a
perceptive article by Renton Laidlaw in the London *Standard* in
which he said the 'ordinary' player does feel a bit more 'special'
now, and that's right.

The journeyman *does* feel he is *someone* these days. He has
first-class equipment, he has the manufacturers' rep bringing
him golf balls, he has access to a courtesy car. And the things
that sponsors are trying, with increasing success, to do all help

towards this – for example, a players' lounge where the newest youngster on the tour may be sitting next to Sevvy. If the novice walks up the steps of the Mizuno caravan two steps ahead of Sevvy, he gets dealt with first and Sevvy second. To some extent it is a psychological boost, but it all helps everyone to feel he is an equal partner in the tour. It's good. It makes us all feel good. The very sight of that bucketful of pristine, white Titleist balls makes you want to stay on the practice ground for an extra hour. Everyone is practising more than used to be the case, so it is no wonder that European standards are racing ahead.

So the competition becomes ever fiercer, year after year, and this is true all the way down the line. Each December we now see more than 200 players sweating out the ordeal of six rounds at La Manga to try to win a precious card to take them into the European tour. It must be a nerve-racking experience – like trying to pre-qualify for The Open, only more so. The most talented golfer can have an off day and turn in a card about ten shots inferior to what he is normally capable of returning. Conversely, a modestly endowed player can have an absolute flyer and produce the sort of score he may not be able to repeat at any time during the year. Six rounds is as good a system as can be evolved to prevent the odd *freak* round from having a wholly decisive effect, and yet inevitably there is always heart-break for someone for whom an unexplained and unidentifiable disaster can mean back-to-the-drawing board for another twelve months. Just fifty places are available from the Qualifying School at La Manga for new faces on the European Tour (or for old faces trying to re-enter) to get into Category 12 of the PGA's exempt list, and that exemption lasts for only one year.

After three tournaments in South Africa in 1988 Andrew Chandler had to fly back to Europe to compete for *his* place (only two years after a third-place finish in the Italian Open, winner the year before that of the Sao Paulo International Classic in Brazil) a professional on the circuit since 1975. Now, once again, he was up against the best young players in the world. They came not only from all parts of Europe but from the USA as well – for instance, Jack Nicklaus junior and the experienced Rick Hartman – and from as far away as Fiji. They included the cream of last season's amateurs now turning to the professional ranks, but there were seasoned pros as well. There are no sinecures, no easy options in professional golf.

The fourth-round cut at La Manga brought its usual crop of heartbreaks. Colin Gillies, assistant at Glenbervie, had a five-under-par inward half which still left him one stroke short of a qualifying score after earlier, less successful rounds. And young Nicklaus perhaps summed up what most players in the field were feeling when he told the *Daily Telegraph*'s Lewine Mair: 'I have never felt less than tense and in that state I don't let myself swing like I know I can swing.' He, too, missed the cut and a lot of us knew exactly how he felt. On the other hand, it must have been an interesting experience for David Jones, twenty-one years a professional, a member of the European Tours Committee and the Irish national coach. Why was he there? He wanted to see if, at forty-one-years-of-age, he could face trying for his card 'amongst all those young whipper-snappers'. He could, he did and he finished joint seventh with rounds of 71-67-74-69-68-73. There was a strong and successful challenge from a whole crop of young Swedes but, alas, when the fifty cards for the 1989 tour were handed out, friend Chandler was not one of the players to receive one.

Every year a new band of hopefuls arrive on the scene to battle for a place against those who have already had a taste of life on the circuit and every year the required degree of excellence in performance is pushed a little higher. I don't want to have to go back to that, nor would I like to return to those grinding days of roaming the courses of Europe, hoping to pre-qualify. At the same time, I would not have missed my formative years on the circuit – not for anything. In their own way, they not only improved my golf but they enriched my life.

Don: It is not difficult to see why standards are improving every year with this sort of competition, but there still must be a lot of good golfers around who do *not* try for a European tour card. There are the club professionals, of course, many of whom venture into competition on only a limited scale, but I am thinking more of the many really gifted amateurs around who, for one reason or another, prefer to remain in the unpaid ranks and yet can still be fiercely competitive. Surely one or two of them must say to themselves from time to time when they look at some of the scores in professional tournaments, 'I think I might have done a bit better than that'?

We have seen that amateurs figure quite regularly in the Open Championship, that they can often put up respectable scores in pro tournaments where they are eligible to compete, and that they can return scores on the more difficult championship courses which are just as respectable as those of pros. What, then, is the essential difference between amateur and professional golf? Is there such a great gap between, say, the general game of the top amateur and the middle-of-the-road pro? If there is, what causes it?

Ian: If you play every week on the tournament circuit, trying to make a living from playing golf, you are forced to find a way of producing a score, irrespective of how you feel and what shape your game happens to be in. That compels you – even those who don't dwell a great deal on technique, and probably I come into that category – to be very much aware all the time of where the ball is going. You have, therefore, to tailor your game to be as good as your *bad* shots and thus there is pressure on you to restrict those bad shots to *conservative* bad shots – to try to confine them to the less disastrous areas of the course.

Don: But isn't that a negative attitude – to accept that you are always going to play a measure of bad shots?

Ian: That may be true, but it is *my* attitude – the way I have always played. I have to play that way. I am not, never will be, in the same league as Ballesteros, Lyle, Faldo and the other top players but at the same time I accept that there are other players on the circuit with a more positive attitude than mine. Towards the end of 1988 I played a round with Des Smyth and I remember being impressed by how positive his attitude was to the game. That sort of approach is based on the belief that what he wants to happen *will* happen; mine is based on an acceptance that what I want to happen might not always happen. But what happens to all of us who play week in, week out, in all sorts of conditions on all types of courses, is that, however positive the attitude is, however confident we feel and however much we want things to go well, we still to some extent become aware of our own fallibility. It is a state of mind which is bound to occur. So long as you live with that you have to organise your mental approach, your course-management and your shot-making with the possibility of error in mind. That means playing the percentage shot.

I think amateurs, even the most accomplished ones, tend to think in terms of the *very best* they can do. This is understandable. If a long and tricky carry is attainable by the *best* shot the amateur is capable of playing he will usually go for it. If the pin position is vulnerable to a soft fade, then he will try the soft fade, even if he is basically a right-to-left player, because it might just come off. If, however, you are playing the game for a living, you work out where the ball *might* finish and the possible consequences of it. Then you plan your shot accordingly – the shot which presents the least likelihood of disaster. If you do that over five or six rounds a week, for thirty-five weeks or more a year, eventually you become more efficient at playing the best shot in all the circumstances. It is, in my view, the pragmatic approach to the game.

Don: But how efficient is that? Do you not think that your attitude is more negative than pragmatic? Does it not explain why you have not won more tournaments than two in Europe and three in South Africa? And what is the difference between you – a journeyman professional, as you describe yourself – and the Lyles, the Faldos, the Woosnams, the Langers and the Ballesteroses – the *winners*?

Ian: A lot of questions there, so let's start with the one which is easiest to answer – the difference between top money-winners and someone in my position. The top players hit the ball thirty or forty yards further than me, so even if all other things were equal, the scale of their game is bigger and therefore they can reduce courses in a way that I can't. And they can do it more often, and thus shoot lower scores more regularly than I am capable of doing. The top ten players now are all enormously long. On top of that they play better golf with crisper striking, more leverage, get the ball higher more quickly, stop it more quickly. They can do more with it. I can do it better than some; others can do it better than me. Basically, there is a disparity in the actual striking of the ball. The gap can be narrowed by a massive amount of work and good coaching, but it can never be closed completely because there is a difference in talent. This is a genuine thing, make no mistake about it. If you play with Sevvy you are aware that he is doing things with the golf ball that you physically cannot do. This is the case even more so with Lyle. I suspect he makes even Sevvy feel ordinary at times, but I would not expect him to admit it. Faldo is perhaps the one who has taken his natural talent and stretched it to the utmost. He may become better than all of them because he is really more dedicated; he *wants* it more and he is really efficient in the way he goes about it.

Turning to the question of why I don't win more tournaments, towards the end of the 1988 season I played in the Equity and Law event at Royal Mid-Surrey with Mark Roe and Derrick Cooper; this is a competition for the highest number of birdies and eagles scored. Mark shot (in stroke-play terms) 61, 61, 64 and Derrick had a similar score. All right, the course was set up for birdies and eagles, but these were still unbelievably low scores and Mark wondered, 'If we played like this all the time, going for birdies and eagles, would we still shoot these low scores?' Barry Lane came back in 26 in one round of that tournament. Everything holed out but it was a genuine medal score and all round the course guys were doing things they would never otherwise do. So I would have to admit that there is a definite attitude-difference there. I don't know whether my attitude will continue to limit the chance that I have to win many tournaments. It probably will. But playing percentages, and understanding what sort of golf-shot you are likely to hit – as opposed to what you would most *like* to hit – is, to me, being professional. It's living with what you have got and what you can do with it.

Instead of thinking, 'the great shot will get me an eagle,' I take the view that I got into more trouble when I was a youngster and wrecked potentially decent scores by being more aggressive and less conservative. I remember a piece of advice I had from Brian Allen when I was very young – and I have always stored away and respected everything he taught me. I had come in after shooting a sub-70 round at Denton and he asked what I had scored. Very pleased with myself, I replied, 'I shot 68.' Unmoved, he asked, 'how did you play?' and I told him, 'Great.' Brian said, 'You *should* shoot 68 when you play great. What can you shoot when you play badly?' I had to think

about it, but then I realised what it is all about. Being a pro
means (a) performing adequately when you don't feel like
playing at all, when you are on a course you don't like, when
you are homesick, when something has upset you and (b) it's
also about producing a score when you are not playing well. I
believe I have improved the bottom end of my game quite a
long way, and maybe I have sacrificed a bit at the top end. In
terms of long-term strategy it is probably too late for me to
become an aggressive, attacking player, but it is a point worth
thinking about, especially bearing in mind our thoughts during
that Equity and Law tournament so recently.

Don: You have had many disappointments in the past
sixteen years, heartbreaks even if we think in terms of the South
African Open. You have had some horrifying experiences in
your travels, lived from hand to mouth, wondered how you
could afford your next tournament. If you were fifteen again
and we were sitting down to talk about your future, would you
opt for a different sort of life?

Ian: Not for one minute. I remember you once saying that
you were lucky in that you had looked forward to going to work
every day of your life and it has been like that for me. I enjoy
most sports, particularly cricket and rugby, and I like a game of
cards or snooker, modern music, films and TV, especially
comedy. I love to laugh. But a very large slice of my life is taken
up with golf. I cannot, for instance, take myself off for a week's
fishing. If I am not playing in a tournament, then during the
day I am either playing a pro–am, a social round or practising.
I am doing what I like best every day of my life and all the year
round. It's sunshine (if we are lucky) all summer and sunshine
through the winter. It's a life in which I have made countless
friends all over the world; I have seen places I could never have
hoped to visit in another job; it's a way of life which, despite its
disappointments and, at times, frustrations, means there is
always something to enjoy in some part of every day. It might
be a meeting with an old friend, or making a new one; it might
be shared laughter, the sight of a spectacular sunset, the first
glimpse of a new course; it might be the satisfaction of a good
shot, painstakingly worked out and successfully executed; it
might lie in the unexpected sighting of wildlife on a course, at

home or abroad; there are a hundred different things which can give delight in the course of a week's golf. And there is pleasure in watching a partner play well, even if your own game is not so good that day. That is one way in which golf stands apart from other games, I believe, much as I enjoy so many other sports. We have respect for each other and for the game we play.

Don: Do you think of it, then, as a gentlemanly game, a sportsmanlike game, even a chivalrous game?

Ian: Unhesitatingly, yes I do. That is the style in which one is brought up to play, and I have always enjoyed it in that way. I think of it in precisely those terms. There have been very, very few rotten apples in golf's barrel over the years, and if anyone should overstep the mark he would be pinpointed and sorted out very quickly indeed. What we are doing is highly competitive in an individual way, but any manifestation of personal animosity is rare in the extreme. We shake hands on the first tee, wish each other luck and then pit our wits and our experience and our ability against the course. But it is not a war and the course is not the enemy. It is a friend we are visiting for the day, a friend with characteristics which have to be understood and appreciated in all their challenging subtleties, and, in a fair and honest contest, to be overcome if possible – all this alongside colleagues who may for the moment be rivals in one sense but who through the entire year are bound together by ties of mutual respect.

I once played alongside Sevvy Ballesteros on his home course in Santander, where, naturally, he had a huge and enthusiastic following. I feared the worst might happen; that if Sevvy putted out first there would be a stampede to the next tee and I would be left to try to sink my ball against a noisy background of scurrying feet and a moving backdrop of rushing figures. I need have had no fears. Sevvy opted to putt out last at every opportunity and held up his arms in what was, from him in that setting, a royal demand for absolute silence when I took my turn. In short, he insisted upon the full observation of the etiquette of the game. He was the greatest player in Europe; I was a simple journeyman, but a colleague. In that moment I was very, very proud to be a member of my chosen profession. I still am, every day.

Index